THE IELTS TREASURY

YOUR COMPLETE GUIDE TO IELTS TOPICS, VOCABULARY & PRACTICE FOR BAND 9 - WRITING & SPEAKING

GAYATHRI JAYAKUMAR

Contents

Table Of Contents

Purpose Of The Book

Purpose of the Book

The IELTS Treasury furnishes learners with a myriad of common topics for IELTS Writing Task 2 and Speaking Part 1 and 3. The book is a treasure trove for students to help familiarize with IELTS' common topics, their question models and get an insight into the kind of words and ideas that can be used. The book is also a guide on how to structure their responses for the essays and is a one-stop solution to ace in their IELTS test. This book will provide the foundation for students to build upon, allowing them to practice, research, and develop their writing and speaking skills confidently and effectively.

Through the course of this book, learners will:

- Explore a wide range of common IELTS Writing Task 2 and Speaking topics.

- Familiarize yourself with key ideas, vocabulary, and concise definitions for each theme.

- Learn how to build strong introductions by using the opening lines provided as adaptable templates.

- Practice developing your responses through sample questions, along with guidance on expanding ideas and addressing subtopics.

Whether you're aiming to strengthen your essays for Writing Task 2 or enhance your performance in the Speaking test, this book is your go-to guide for mastering topic familiarity, response structure, and answer refinement — all to help you reach a higher band score.

How To Use This Book

1. **Get to Know the Topics**
   Each topic includes a sample question to show how it might appear in the IELTS exam. Review these to understand common themes and question styles.

2. **Master Introductions**
   The opening lines provided under *Core Topics* are designed as flexible templates for Writing Task 2 introductions. Use them as a starting point and adapt them to suit specific prompts.

3. **Deepen Your Knowledge**
   Use the ideas and subtopics in each section as a foundation for further research. Building topic-specific vocabulary and expanding your understanding will help you craft more convincing, well-developed responses.

4. **Practice Writing**
   Write responses to the sample questions after studying the material. Regular practice will improve both your writing quality and speed. Be mindful of timing as you work towards exam readiness.

5. **Prepare for Speaking**
   Many topics also appear in IELTS Speaking Part 3. Use them to practice organizing your thoughts and speaking fluently under time pressure.

Sample of Introduction for Writing Task 2 Topic - Happiness:

" Happiness, a state of emotional well-being registered by feelings of contentment, joy, and satisfaction comes from multiple causes like personal achievements, relationships, or simply a sense of inner peace. (Paraphrase the question in 1 or 2 sentences). The following paragraphs will elaborate on these ideas."

By applying this structure, you can quickly frame your introduction with clarity, making your answer more organized and precise. Expand from this introduction with well-supported body paragraphs, detailing your stance, relevant examples, and counterarguments when necessary and end with a conclusion that summarises your introduction and body paragraphs.

Abstract Concepts for IELTS (Core List)

CHAPTER I

Abstract Concepts

These are the most difficult topics as it gets extremely difficult work on such abstract concepts in the heat of the test. Most people go blank with these topics and struggle with points to address the questions.

1. **Happiness:**

Happiness, a state of emotional well-being registered by feelings of contentment, joy, and satisfaction comes from multiple causes. Some of these are personal achievements, relationships, health, or simply a sense of purpose and inner peace.

10 Points You Can Use in IELTS Answers (Writing/Speaking)

1. Happiness means different things to different people — for some, it's financial stability; for others, it's meaningful relationships.

1. Long-term happiness is often linked to personal values and purpose rather than material possessions.

3. Mental and physical health play a vital role in a person's overall happiness.

4. Countries like Bhutan focus on Gross National Happiness rather than GDP.

5. Strong family ties and social connections contribute significantly to our mental well-being.

6. Too much focus on external success may lead to temporary satisfaction but not true happiness.

7. Gratitude and mindfulness practices have been shown to improve happiness levels.

8. Work-life balance is essential for maintaining emotional well-being.

9. Personal freedom and self-sufficiency are closely associated with happiness in many cultures.

10. Governments can play a role by investing in mental health services and community welfare.

10 Useful Words for IELTS Answers

   I. Well-being

  II. Contentment

 III. Satisfaction

 IV. Fulfillment

  V. Joy

 VI. Gratitude

VII. Positivity

VIII. Mental health

 IX. Balance

  X. Inner peace

Synonyms / Related Words

- Contentment
- Fulfillment
- Well-being

IELTS Writing Task 2 – Q type : Opinion Question with Example-

Some people believe that happiness depends more on external circumstances such as income and social status, while others argue it is influenced mainly by individual mindset and values.

Discuss both views and give your opinion. Provide examples where relevant.

2. **Intelligence:**

Intelligence is the ability to acquire and apply knowledge and skills. It includes logical thinking, problem-solving, creativity, emotional understanding, and adaptability — not just academic or technical ability.

10 Points You Can Use in IELTS Answers (Writing/Speaking)

1. Intelligence is multi-dimensional — it can be emotional, social, creative, or logical.

2. IQ tests measure only certain aspects, mainly logical and mathematical intelligence.

3. Emotional intelligence (EQ) is essential in teamwork, leadership, and relationships.

4. In education, schools often overlook creative and interpersonal intelligence.

5. Artificial Intelligence is reshaping how we define and understand human intelligence.

6. Some people argue intelligence is innate, while others believe it is shaped by environment and experience.

7. Intelligence alone does not guarantee success; discipline and social skills also matter.

8. Different cultures may value different forms of intelligence (e.g., academic vs. practical).

9. Intelligence can be nurtured over time through learning and life experiences.

10. Technological advancements have created new types of intelligence, like digital literacy.

10 Useful Words for IELTS Answers

I. IQ

II. EQ (Emotional Intelligence)

III. Problem-solving

IV. Critical thinking

V. Adaptability

VI. Creativity
VII. Cognitive skills

VIII. Logic

IX. Innovation

X. Analytical thinking

Synonyms / Related Words

- Cognition
- Smartness
- Mental ability

IELTS Writing Task 2 – Q type : Advantage-Disadvantage Outweigh Question-
Some people believe that measuring intelligence through standardized tests is beneficial, while others think it limits a person's potential.

Do the advantages of standardized intelligence tests outweigh the disadvantages?

.

3. Success:

Success is the achievement of personal, academic, or professional goals. It can be defined differently by individuals — for some, it's wealth and status; for others, it's personal fulfillment, stability, or impact on others.

10 Points You Can Use in IELTS Answers (Writing/Speaking)

1. Success is subjective — it means different things to different people.

2. Many people associate success with money, career, or social recognition.

3. Others view success as achieving personal happiness or life balance.

4. Hard work, consistency, and perseverance are often seen as key factors.

5. External factors like luck, opportunity, or social connections also play a role.

6. Failure is often a stepping stone toward long-term success.

7. The media and society may create unrealistic standards of success.

8. Education is traditionally seen as a path to success, though not always necessary.

9. Work-life balance is increasingly considered part of a successful life.

10. Success without personal satisfaction or mental peace may feel hollow.

10 Useful Words for IELTS Answers

I. Achievement

II. Ambition

III. Fulfillment

IV. Determination

 V. Wealth

VI. Recognition

VII. Career

VIII. Goals

IX. Motivation

 X. Self-discipline

Synonyms / Related Words

- Achievement
- Accomplishment
- Fulfillment

IELTS Writing Task 2 – Q type : Cause and Effect Question-
Many young people today are under pressure to be successful at an early age.
What are the causes of this trend? What are its effects on individuals and society?

4. **Freedom :**

Freedom is the ability to act, speak, or think without unnecessary restrictions. It can refer to personal liberty, political rights, freedom of expression, or freedom from oppression or control.
10 Points You Can Use in IELTS Answers (Writing/Speaking)

1. Freedom is a core value in many democratic societies, associated with human rights.
2. It includes freedom of speech, religion, movement, and choice.

3. Too much freedom without responsibility can lead to chaos or social harm.
4. Freedom of the press is essential for transparency and democracy.
5. In some countries, freedom is restricted due to political control or cultural norms.
6. Social media has raised questions about freedom of expression versus misinformation.
7. Economic freedom, such as the ability to choose jobs or start businesses, is vital for growth.
8. Freedom often comes with limits for the sake of national security or public safety.
9. History shows that people have fought wars and revolutions in pursuit of freedom.
10. Balancing freedom with laws and social order is a constant challenge for governments.

10 Useful Words for IELTS Answers

I. Liberty

II. Rights

III. Autonomy

IV. Expression

V. Censorship

VI. Democracy

VII. Oppression

VIII. Individuality

IX. Civil liberties

X. Sovereignty

Synonyms / Related Words

- Liberty
- Autonomy
- Independence

IELTS Writing Task 2 – Q type : Agree/Disagree with Example-
Some people believe that freedom of speech should be unlimited, while others argue that it must be restricted to protect individuals and society.

Do you agree or disagree with this statement? Give reasons for your answer and include examples from your own knowledge or experience.

5. **Justice:**

Justice refers to the principle of fairness where individuals receive equal treatment and outcomes are based on truth, law, and ethics. It includes legal justice, social justice, and moral accountability.

10 Points You Can Use in IELTS Answers (Writing/Speaking)

1. Justice ensures people are treated equally, regardless of background or status.
2. Legal systems are designed to uphold justice through laws and courts.
3. Social justice focuses on equality in education, healthcare, and opportunities.
4. Corruption can prevent true justice from being served.
5. Justice must be impartial, with fair trials and protection of individual rights.
6. Injustice can lead to protests, unrest, or even revolutions.
7. Justice systems differ across cultures — some value rehabilitation, others punishment.
8. Technology like body cameras or digital evidence can support justice.
9. Justice delayed is often justice denied — efficiency is essential in courts.
10. Education and awareness are crucial for building a just society.

10 Useful Words for IELTS Answers

I. Fairness

II.   Equality

III.   Law

IV.   Rights

V.   Accountability

VI.   Court

VII.   Rule of law

VIII.   Corruption

IX.   Punishment

X.   Rehabilitation

Synonyms / Related Words

- Fairness
- Lawfulness
- Impartiality

IELTS Writing Task 2 – Q type: Advantage-Disadvantage Opinion Question-

Some people think that harsh punishments are necessary to maintain justice, while others believe rehabilitation is more effective.

Discuss the advantages and disadvantages of both approaches and give your opinion

6.   **Equality:**

Equality is the principle that all individuals should be treated fairly and have the same opportunities, regardless of their gender, race, economic background, or social status.

10 Points You Can Use in IELTS Answers (Writing/Speaking)

1. Equality in education ensures that all students have access to learning, regardless of their background.
2. Gender equality promotes equal rights, responsibilities, and opportunities for men and women.
3. Economic inequality often leads to social tension and limits upward mobility.
4. Equal pay for equal work is a key issue in many countries.
5. Laws promoting equality help protect minorities and marginalized groups.
6. True equality goes beyond law — it requires a change in mindset and culture.
7. In many workplaces, there is still a lack of representation in leadership roles.
8. Technology can either bridge or widen the equality gap depending on access.
9. Equality is essential for a just and harmonious society.
10. Promoting equality fosters diversity, innovation, and productivity.

10 Useful Words for IELTS Answers

I. Fairness

II. Inclusion

III. Discrimination

IV. Equity

V. Diversity

VI. Rights

VII. Opportunity

VIII. Representation

IX. Bias

X. Marginalization

Synonyms / Related Words

- Equity
- Fairness
- Impartiality

IELTS Writing Task 2 – Q type : To What Extent Do You Agree/ Disagree-

Equality in the workplace is achievable only through strict government regulation.

To what extent do you agree or disagree with this statement?

.

7. **Love:**

Love is a deep affection towards someone or something. It can be romantic, familial, platonic, or even a passion for an activity or idea. It plays a vital role in human relationships and emotional well-being.

10 Points You Can Use in IELTS Answers (Writing/Speaking)

1. Love contributes to emotional well-being and can reduce stress and anxiety.
2. Family love is often the first source of emotional support and security.
3. Romantic love is frequently portrayed in media, influencing societal expectations.
4. Cultures differ in how they express and value love in relationships.
5. Love and emotional connection are key to strong marriages and long-term partnerships.
6. In some societies, arranged marriages prioritize compatibility over romantic love.
7. Acts of love, such as kindness and sacrifice, strengthen communities.
8. Love for a career, hobby, or cause can drive personal motivation and fulfillment.
9. Technology has changed how people find and express love (e.g., dating apps, virtual communication).

10. Excessive attachment or unhealthy love can lead to emotional dependence and imbalance.

10 Useful Words for IELTS Answers

    I. Affection

   II. Attachment

  III. Bond

  IV. Emotion

    V. Intimacy

  VI. Compassion

 VII. Devotion

VIII. Relationship

  IX. Connection

   X. Sacrifice

Synonyms / Related Words

- Affection
- Devotion
- Adoration

IELTS Writing Task 2 – Q type : Double Question with Example-
Why is love important in human relationships? What challenges can arise when love is absent in families or society?
Use examples from your own knowledge or experience to support your answer.

8. **Trust:**

Trust is the belief in the reliability, honesty, or integrity of a person, organization, or system. It forms the foundation of strong relationships and is essential for cooperation and social harmony.

10 Points You Can Use in IELTS Answers (Writing/Speaking)

1. Trust is essential for maintaining healthy relationships, whether personal or professional.

2. A lack of trust can lead to conflict, insecurity, or breakdown in communication.

3. In business, trust between companies and consumers influences brand loyalty.

4. Political trust affects how citizens respond to government policies and leadership.

5. Trust must be built over time and can be easily lost through dishonesty or betrayal.

6. Trust is the basis of all relationships.

7. Trust in media is decreasing in many countries due to misinformation and bias.

8. Online transactions and digital services rely heavily on user trust.

9. Social trust contributes to safer, more cooperative communities.

10. Transparency and accountability are key to rebuilding trust when it's broken.

10 Useful Words for IELTS Answers

I. Reliability

II. Honesty

III.   Integrity

IV.   Loyalty

 V.   Transparency

VI.   Faith

VII.   Dependability

VIII.   Cooperation

 IX.   Credibility

  X.   Reputation

Synonyms / Related Words

- Reliability
- Confidence
- Faith

IELTS Writing Task 2 – Q type : Problem-Solution Question-
In recent years, there has been a noticeable decline in public trust towards governments and large corporations.
What are the causes of this decline? What measures can be taken to rebuild trust?

9.   **Honesty**

Honesty is the quality of being truthful, sincere, and free from deceit. It involves telling the truth, keeping promises, and being fair in actions and decisions.
10 Points You Can Use in IELTS Answers (Writing/Speaking)

1.   Honesty is a key value in personal relationships, fostering trust and respect.

2. In education, academic honesty helps maintain fairness and integrity.

3. Workplace honesty promotes transparency, accountability, and ethical practices.

4. Dishonesty can lead to serious consequences, such as legal action or damaged reputation.

5. Children often learn the value of honesty from parents and early education.

6. Political honesty is vital for public trust in leaders and institutions.

7. Cultural views on honesty may differ — some prioritize politeness over full truth.

8. Technology, like lie detectors and digital tracking, raises new questions about honesty and privacy.

9. Being honest can be difficult in situations involving fear, shame, or social pressure.

10. Honesty in media and journalism is critical for an informed society.

10 Useful Words for IELTS Answers

I. Integrity

II. Transparency

III. Sincerity

IV. Truthfulness

V. Morality

VI. Ethics

VII.   Authenticity

VIII. Accountability

IX.   Fairness

X.   Trustworthiness

Synonyms / Related Words

- Truthfulness
- Integrity
- Sincerity

IELTS Writing Task 2 – Q type : Opinion Question -
Some people believe that honesty is always the best policy, while others argue that being too honest can cause harm in certain situations.
What is your opinion on this matter?

10. **Truth:**

Truth is the state of being in accordance with fact or reality involving honesty, accuracy, and authenticity in communication and behavior.
10 Points You Can Use in IELTS Answers (Writing/Speaking)

1. Truth is a foundation of trust in relationships, education, and governance.

2. In journalism and media, delivering the truth is essential for an informed society.

3. Truth can sometimes be uncomfortable but is necessary for progress and justice.

4. Social media often blurs the line between truth and opinion or misinformation.

5. Truthfulness in education supports critical thinking and intellectual integrity.

6. Cultural and individual perspectives may affect what is considered "truth."

7. Legal systems depend on uncovering the truth to deliver fair judgments.

8. Sometimes, people withhold the truth to avoid hurting others or facing consequences.

9. Scientific truth is based on evidence and is constantly evolving through research.

10. Promoting truth in leadership helps maintain public trust and ethical governance.

10 Useful Words for IELTS Answers

I. Accuracy

II. Authenticity

III. Honesty

IV. Evidence

V. Transparency

VI. Clarity

VII. Integrity

VIII. Objectivity

IX. Misinformation

X. Reality

Synonyms / Related Words

- Reality
- Fact
- Veracity

IELTS Writing Task 2 – Q type : agree or disagree Question -
It is sometimes argued that telling the truth is not always the best option in certain situations.
Do you agree or disagree with this statement?

11. **Hope:**

Hope is the optimistic feeling or belief that something good will happen in the future, especially during challenging times.
10 Points You Can Use in IELTS Answers (Writing/Speaking)

1. Hope is essential for emotional resilience during difficult situations.

2. It motivates people to keep working towards their goals despite setbacks.

3. Societies often promote hope through education, religion, and social values.

4. Hope contributes positively to mental health and well-being.

5. Hope is the driving factor for most people to move forward in life despite the challenges they face every day.

6. People who maintain hope tend to cope better with stress and failure.

7. Communities affected by disasters rely on hope to rebuild and recover.

8. Hope can be a driving force in social movements and political change.

9. Children raised in hopeful environments tend to have stronger self-esteem.

10. Literature and films often portray hope as a central human value.

10 Useful Words for IELTS Answers

I. Optimism

II. Motivation

III. Resilience

IV. Perseverance

V. Positivity

VI. Ambition

VII. Aspiration

VIII. Inspiration

IX. Future-oriented

X. Determination

Synonyms / Related Words

- Faith – belief without proof; trust in something better
- Optimism – a positive outlook on future outcomes
- Expectation – belief that something will occur

IELTS Writing Task 2 – Q type : Advantage–Disadvantage outweigh
Question-
Some people believe that having hope during difficult times is essential, while others think it can lead to unrealistic expectations.
What are the advantages and disadvantages of having hope? Do you think the advantages outweigh the disadvantages?

12. **Fear:**

Fear is an emotional response to perceived danger or threat, which can influence thoughts, behavior, and decision-making.

10 Points You Can Use in IELTS Answers (Writing/Speaking)

1. Fear is a natural and protective emotion that helps humans avoid danger.

2. It can be both rational (real threats) and irrational (phobias or anxiety).

3. Fear can motivate people to take precautions or prepare better.

4. In extreme cases, it may lead to paralysis, inaction, or poor decisions.

5. Governments sometimes use fear in public safety campaigns (e.g., smoking warnings).

6. Fear of failure can push individuals to work harder or, conversely, avoid trying.

7. Fear can negatively impact mental health if not managed properly.

8. Social fear, such as fear of judgment, can limit personal growth.

9. Media often amplifies fear, especially during crises or disasters.

10. Learning to manage fear is essential for personal development and success.

10 Useful Words for IELTS Answers

I. Anxiety

II. Phobia

III. Risk

IV. Threat

V. Panic

VI.   Caution

VII.   Avoidance

VIII.   Stress

IX.   Trauma

X.   Insecurity

Synonyms / Related Words

- Dread
- Alarm
- Apprehension

IELTS Writing Task 2 – Q type Cause and Effect Question -
Why do people experience fear in certain situations, and what effects can it have on their behavior?.

13. **Courage:**

Courage is the ability to face fear, danger, or adversity despite feeling afraid or uncertain.
10 Points You Can Use in IELTS Answers (Writing/Speaking)

1. Courage is often required to take risks and make difficult decisions.

2. It can be physical (e.g., firefighters) or moral (e.g., standing up for what's right).

3. People with courage often inspire others and become role models.

4. Courage helps individuals overcome fear and move forward in life.

5. Acts of courage are essential in leadership and crisis situations.

6. Courage is not the absence of fear but the decision to act despite it.

7. Speaking out against injustice is a common example of moral courage.

8. Students and young people show courage by pursuing dreams despite obstacles.

9. Cultural stories and media often highlight courageous characters.

10. Courage can be developed through experience, support, and self-belief.

10 Useful Words for IELTS Answers

I. Bravery

II. Valor

III. Resolve

IV. Risk-taking

V. Resilience

VI. Grit

VII. Determination

VIII. Heroism

IX. Tenacity

X. Integrity

Synonyms / Related Words

- Bravery
- Fearlessness
- Fortitude

IELTS Writing Task 2 – Q type : Agree/Disagree with Example Question-

Some people believe that courage is a natural trait, while others think it can be learned.

Do you agree or disagree? Provide reasons and examples to support your opinion.

14. Respect:

Respect is showing consideration, admiration, or regard for someone or something, often reflected in behavior and language.

10 Points You Can Use in IELTS Answers (Writing/Speaking)

1. Respect is fundamental for maintaining healthy personal and professional relationships.

2. It encourages open-mindedness and tolerance in diverse societies.

3. Respecting elders and traditions is deeply rooted in many cultures.

4. Schools play a vital role in teaching children how to respect others.

5. A lack of respect can lead to conflict, misunderstandings, and social tension.

6. Respect at the workplace boosts teamwork and employee morale.

7. Mutual respect strengthens communication and cooperation.

8. Online interactions have raised concerns about declining respectful behavior.

9. Respect for nature is crucial for promoting sustainable living.

10. Leaders gain trust and loyalty when they treat others with respect.

10 Useful Words for IELTS Answers

I.   Courtesy

II.   Politeness

III.   Tolerance

IV.   Manners

V.   Civility

VI.   Recognition

VII.   Consideration

VIII.   Deference

IX.   Esteem

X.   Dignity

Synonyms / Related Words

- Admiration
- Honour
- Regard

IELTS Writing Task 2 – Q type : Double Question with Example-
Why is respect important in today's society? How can individuals show respect in everyday situations?
Give examples to support your answer.

15. **Confidence:**

Confidence is the belief in one's own abilities, qualities, or judgment, often reflected in how someone acts or communicates.
10 Points You Can Use in IELTS Answers (Writing/Speaking)

1. Confidence plays a key role in personal and professional success.

2. People with confidence are often more willing to take risks and try new things.

3. Self-confidence can improve public speaking and communication skills.

4. Education and supportive environments help build confidence in children.

5. Lack of confidence can lead to missed opportunities and underachievement.

6. Confidence is essential in leadership and decision-making roles.

7. Overconfidence, however, can lead to poor judgment or arrogance.

8. Confidence can be developed through experience, practice, and feedback.

9. Social media can both boost and harm people's confidence depending on usage.

10. Confidence contributes to better mental health and self-esteem.

10 Useful Words for IELTS Answers

I. Self-esteem

II. Assurance

III. Positivity

IV. Boldness

V. Assertiveness

VI. Empowerment

VII. Motivation

VIII. Growth mindset

IX. Independence

X. Charisma

Synonyms / Related Words

- Self- assurance
- Certainty
- Sel-belief

IELTS Writing Task 2 – Q type : Problem–Solution Question-
Many people struggle with low self-confidence, which affects their personal and professional lives.
What problems can low confidence cause, and what are some effective solutions?

16. **Creativity:**

Creativity is one's ability to generate original ideas, think outside the box, or find innovative solutions to problems.
10 Points You Can Use in IELTS Answers (Writing/Speaking)

1. Creativity is essential in fields like art, design, and technology.

2. It drives innovation and progress in science, business, and education.

3. Children develop creativity through play, exploration, and arts.

4. Creative thinking improves problem-solving and adaptability.

5. Schools that encourage creativity often produce more engaged learners.

6. Many successful entrepreneurs rely on creativity to build unique products or services.

7. Creative individuals often contribute to cultural and social development.

8. Creativity is not limited to artists; it applies to all professions.

9. Modern workplaces seek employees who can think creatively and independently.

10. Lack of creative freedom can lead to monotony and reduced motivation.

10 Useful Words for IELTS Answers

I. Innovation

II. Imagination

III. Originality

IV. Brainstorming

V. Expression

VI. Invention

VII. Visionary

VIII. Flexibility

IX. Intuition

X. Ingenuity

Synonyms / Related Words

- Innovation
- Imagination
- Inventiveness

IELTS Writing Task 2 – Q type : Opinion Question with Example-
Some people believe that creativity is a natural talent, while others think it can be developed through practice.

What is your opinion? Give reasons and examples to support your answer.

17. **Wisdom:**

Wisdom is the ability to use knowledge, experience, and good judgment to make thoughtful and informed decisions.
10 Points You Can Use in IELTS Answers (Writing/Speaking)

1. Wisdom is often gained over time through life experiences and reflection.

2. It goes beyond intelligence and involves understanding long-term consequences.

3. Wise individuals are often respected in society for their guidance and insight.

4. Wisdom plays a key role in ethical decision-making and conflict resolution.

5. Elderly people are commonly viewed as wise due to their accumulated experiences.

6. Wisdom helps people navigate complex social or moral issues.

7. Education and open-mindedness can contribute to developing wisdom.

8. Cultures and religions often value wisdom as a core virtue.

9. Leaders who act with wisdom tend to be more trusted and effective.

10. Wisdom can be seen in actions that balance logic, emotion, and ethics.

10 Useful Words for IELTS Answers

I. Insight

II.   Judgment

III. Experience

IV.   Maturity

V.   Discernment

VI.   Prudence

VII. Understanding

VIII. Intuition

IX.   Knowledge

X.   Perspective

Synonyms / Related Words

- Insight
- Prudence
- Acumen

IELTS Writing Task 2 – Q type : to what extent do you agree/disagree- Wisdom is more important than intelligence in making life decisions. **To what extent do you agree or disagree with this statement?**

18. **Knowledge:**

Knowledge is the information, understanding, and skills that a person gains through education, experience, or study.
10 Points You Can Use in IELTS Answers (Writing/Speaking)

1. Knowledge is essential for personal growth and informed decision-making.

2. Formal education is a primary way to acquire academic knowledge.

3. Practical knowledge often comes from real-life experiences and challenges.

4. In the modern world, access to knowledge has been transformed by the internet.

5. Knowledge-sharing improves societies and drives innovation.

6. A knowledgeable workforce is crucial for national development.

7. There's a growing debate between the value of theoretical vs. practical knowledge.

8. Lifelong learning helps individuals remain competitive in their careers.

9. Knowledge can empower people and reduce inequality.

10. With great knowledge comes responsibility in how it is used.

10 Useful Words for IELTS Answers

I. Information

II. Understanding

III. Awareness

IV. Education

V. Intelligence

VI. Expertise

VII. Insight

VIII. Learning

IX. Wisdom

X. Comprehension

Synonyms / Related Words

- Understanding
- Expertise
- Awareness

IELTS Writing Task 2 – Q type : Advantage–Disadvantage Opinion Question-

Gaining knowledge from books is often considered more valuable than learning from experience.
What are the advantages and disadvantages of learning from books? Do you think it is better than learning through experience?.

19. **Friendship:**

Friendship is a close and trusting relationship between two or more people, often built on mutual respect, support, and shared experiences.
10 Points You Can Use in IELTS Answers (Writing/Speaking)

1. Friendship contributes significantly to emotional well-being and mental health.

2. True friends offer support during difficult times and celebrate during successes.

3. Friendships help individuals feel valued, reducing feelings of loneliness.

4. Social skills such as communication and empathy are developed through friendships.

5. Long-term friendships often require effort, trust, and compromise.

6. Technology and social media have changed how people form and maintain friendships.

7. Cultural values influence how people view and prioritize friendships.

8. Childhood friendships play a key role in social development.

9. Conflicts in friendships can help people grow emotionally if resolved positively.

10. Friendships across different cultures promote understanding and global harmony.

10 Useful Words for IELTS Answers

I. Bond

II. Trust

III. Loyalty

IV. Companionship

V. Affection

VI. Support

VII. Understanding

VIII. Reliability

IX. Intimacy

X. Connection

Synonyms / Related Words

- Companionship
- Camaraderie
- Closeness

IELTS Writing Task 2 – Q type : Single Opinion Question-

Do you think it is more important to have many friends or a few close ones? Why?.

20. **Motivation:**

Motivation is the internal drive or desire that pushes individuals to take action, achieve goals, or pursue ambitions, often influenced by personal values or external rewards.

10 Points You Can Use in IELTS Answers (Writing/Speaking)

1. Motivation is crucial for personal success and achieving long-term goals.

2. It can come from internal sources (intrinsic) or external factors (extrinsic).

3. Intrinsic motivation comes from personal satisfaction, while extrinsic motivation is driven by rewards or recognition.

4. Setting clear, achievable goals often enhances motivation and focus.

5. Positive reinforcement and encouragement can increase motivation levels.

6. Motivation can fluctuate depending on the task, environment, or individual mindset.

7. Lack of motivation can lead to procrastination and poor performance.

8. Teachers and mentors can play a key role in inspiring and motivating others.

9. Motivation is often linked to self-discipline and perseverance in the face of challenges.

10. In workplaces, motivation impacts productivity, job satisfaction, and employee retention.

10 Useful Words for IELTS Answers

I. Drive

II. Determination

III. Ambition

IV. Incentive

V. Encouragement

VI. Passion

VII. Persistence

VIII. Willpower

IX. Commitment

X. Enthusiasm

Synonyms / Related Words

- Inspiration
- zeal
- Encouragement

IELTS Writing Task 2 – Q type Advantage-Disadvantage Opinion Question-

Some people believe that financial rewards are the best way to motivate employees, while others think that non-financial factors, such as job satisfaction, are more effective.

What are the advantages and disadvantages of each approach? Which one do you think is more effective?

21. **Ambition:**

Ambition is a strong desire to achieve something, typically requiring hard work, determination, and a clear goal.

10 Points You Can Use in IELTS Answers (Writing/Speaking)

1. Ambition motivates individuals to set and pursue challenging goals.

2. Ambitious people are often driven to improve themselves and their circumstances.

3. Ambition can lead to personal and professional growth through hard work and perseverance.

4. While ambition can lead to success, it may also cause stress or unhealthy competition.

5. It is important to balance ambition with well-being to avoid burnout.

6. Ambition can be influenced by cultural and societal expectations.

7. Not everyone is motivated by ambition; some people are content with a simpler life.

8. Ambition often pushes individuals to take risks in order to achieve greater rewards.

9. Parents and mentors can inspire ambition by encouraging children to aim high.

10. Some view ambition as a necessary trait for leadership and innovation.

10 Useful Words for IELTS Answers

I. Drive

II. Determination

III. Goal-setting

IV. Perseverance

   V. Aspiration

  VI. Success

 VII. Motivation

VIII. Achievement

  IX. Vision

   X. Self-improvement

Synonyms / Related Words

- Aspiration
- Drive
- Desire

IELTS Writing Task 2 – Q type : Cause and Effect Question-
What are the causes of ambition, and how does it affect a person's life?

22. **Responsibility:**

Responsibility refers to the duty or obligation to take care of something or someone, and being accountable for one's actions and decisions.
10 Points You Can Use in IELTS Answers (Writing/Speaking)

1. Responsibility is a key factor in personal growth and accountability.

2. Everyone has responsibilities, whether at home, at school, or in the workplace.

3. Taking responsibility leads to increased trust and respect from others.

4. Parents often teach their children about responsibility from a young age.

5. Having responsibility can help individuals develop time management and organizational skills.

6. In the workplace, employees are responsible for completing their tasks efficiently.

7. Lack of responsibility can lead to problems such as mistakes or poor performance.

8. Responsibility involves not only fulfilling duties but also being answerable for the outcomes.

9. The growing reliance on technology has shifted some responsibilities in modern society.

10. Responsibility can create a sense of purpose and fulfillment, as people feel they are contributing to something greater.

10 Useful Words for IELTS Answers

I. Accountability

II. Duty

III. Obligation

IV. Commitment

V. Dependability

VI. Ownership

VII. Role

VIII. Liability

IX. Trustworthiness

X. Answerability

Synonyms / Related Words

- Accountability
- Duty
- Obligation

IELTS Writing Task 2 – Q type : Advantage-Disadvantage Opinion Question-
Some people believe that having personal responsibility for one's actions is important, while others think it is more important to share responsibility with others.
What are the advantages and disadvantages of each viewpoint? Which one do you think is more effective?

23. **Loyalty:**

Loyalty is the quality of being faithful, supportive, and committed to someone, something, or a cause, often based on trust and mutual respect.
10 Points You Can Use in IELTS Answers (Writing/Speaking)

1. Loyalty is important in personal relationships, fostering trust and stability.

2. It can be seen in friendships, family bonds, and romantic partnerships.

3. Loyalty is often valued in the workplace, where employees show dedication to their company.

4. A loyal person is usually dependable, showing support even during difficult times.

5. Loyalty can also extend to brands or products, where customers consistently choose the same service or item.

6. In some cultures, loyalty is considered a virtue, and it is emphasized in social interactions.

7. Loyalty may sometimes lead to blind allegiance, which can be problematic if it causes harm or leads to poor judgment.

8. Loyalty is often tested in challenging situations, such as conflicts or disagreements.

9. Loyalty can help build strong communities where individuals look out for one another.

10. However, loyalty should be reciprocal to be truly meaningful and beneficial.

10 Useful Words for IELTS Answers

    I. Faithfulness

   II. Commitment

  III. Allegiance

  IV. Devotion

   V. Support

  VI. Dedication

 VII. Trust

VIII. Reliability

  IX. Attachment

   X. Fidelity

Synonyms / Related Words

- Faithfulness
- Allegiance
- Devotion

IELTS Writing Task 2 – Q type : To what extent do you agree or disagree Question -

Some people argue that loyalty to a group or organization is more important than individual freedom.

To what extent do you agree or disagree with this statement?.

24. **Empathy:**

Empathy is the ability to understand and share the feelings, thoughts, and experiences of another person from their perspective.

10 Points You Can Use in IELTS Answers (Writing/Speaking)

1. Empathy plays a vital role in building strong interpersonal relationships.

2. It helps people connect on a deeper emotional level.

3. Empathetic individuals are often better at resolving conflicts.

4. Empathy fosters kindness, tolerance, and social harmony.

5. It is essential in professions like healthcare, education, and counseling.

6. Empathy can reduce prejudice and promote inclusion in diverse societies.

7. It can be developed through active listening and open-mindedness.

8. Technology and fast-paced life may reduce opportunities for real empathy.

9. Teaching empathy in schools can lead to more emotionally intelligent generations.

10. Lack of empathy may result in bullying, discrimination, or emotional disconnect.

10 Useful Words for IELTS Answers

I. Compassion

II. Understanding

III. Sympathy

IV. Tolerance

V. Sensitivity

VI. Kindness

VII. Respect

VIII. Emotional intelligence

IX. Support

X. Perspective

Synonyms / Related Words

- Compassion
- Sensitivity
- Understanding

IELTS Writing Task 2 – Q type : Cause and Effect Question-
Why is empathy becoming more important in modern society, and what effects can it have on individuals and communities?

25. **Kindness:**

Kindness is the quality of being friendly, generous, and considerate toward others without expecting anything in return.
10 Points You Can Use in IELTS Answers (Writing/Speaking)

1. Kindness strengthens human connections and promotes social harmony.

2. Simple acts of kindness can improve someone's day or emotional well-being.

3. Kindness is essential in both personal and professional relationships.

4. It encourages empathy and understanding in diverse communities.

5. Schools and parents play a key role in teaching children to be kind.

6. Kind behavior often inspires others to act similarly, creating a positive ripple effect.

7. Practicing kindness can improve mental health by reducing stress and increasing happiness.

8. In workplaces, kindness fosters teamwork, respect, and better communication.

9. Social media campaigns often promote kindness as a way to combat bullying and hate.

10. Though often underestimated, kindness is a powerful tool for societal change.

10 Useful Words for IELTS Answers

I. Generosity

II. Compassion

III. Thoughtfulness

IV. Altruism

V. Respect

VI. Humility

VII. Caring

VIII. Supportiveness

IX. Courtesy

X. Humanity

Synonyms / Related Words

- Compassion
- Altruism
- Thoughtfulness

IELTS Writing Task 2 – Q type : Opinion Question with Example-
Some people believe that kindness is a natural human trait, while others think it must be taught.
What is your opinion? Give relevant reason and examples from your knowledge or experience.

26. **Discipline:**

Discipline is the practice of training oneself or others to follow rules, maintain self-control, and behave in a structured, responsible manner.
10 Points You Can Use in IELTS Answers (Writing/Speaking)

1. Discipline is essential for achieving long-term goals and personal growth.

2. It teaches self-control, time management, and consistency.

3. Students with discipline tend to perform better academically.

4. Discipline in the workplace leads to better productivity and professionalism.

5. It helps individuals resist distractions and stay focused.

6. Lack of discipline can lead to poor habits and missed opportunities.

7. Discipline is often instilled through routines, structure, and consequences.

8. Parental guidance plays a vital role in teaching discipline at an early age.

9. Societies with strong discipline often function more smoothly and efficiently.

10. Discipline is not about punishment but about creating a framework for success.

10 Useful Words for IELTS Answers

I. Self-control

II. Routine

III. Consistency

IV. Focus

V. Regulation

VI. Responsibility

VII. Order

VIII. Obedience

IX. Punctuality

X. Determination

Synonyms / Related Words

- Self-discipline
- Control
- Orderliness

IELTS Writing Task 2 – Q type : Advantage–Disadvantage Question-
Discipline is often considered an essential quality in both personal and professional life.
What are the advantages and disadvantages of being highly disciplined?

27. Curiosity:

Curiosity is a strong desire to learn, understand, or explore something new.

10 Points You Can Use in IELTS Answers (Writing/Speaking)

1. Curiosity is the foundation of learning and discovery.

2. It drives innovation and scientific breakthroughs.

3. Curious individuals often ask questions and seek deeper understanding.

4. Children are naturally curious, which helps their cognitive development.

5. Encouraging curiosity in schools can lead to more engaged and independent learners.

6. Curiosity can lead to problem-solving and creative thinking.

7. Excessive curiosity, if not guided, can lead to distractions or risky behavior.

8. Curiosity helps people adapt to new environments and challenges.

9. In the workplace, curiosity can lead to improved performance and innovation.

10. Lifelong curiosity supports personal growth and a love for learning..

10 Useful Words for IELTS Answers

I. Inquiry

II. Exploration

III. Imagination

IV. Innovation

V. Discovery

VI. Engagement

VII. Open-mindedness

VIII. Intelligence

IX. Wonder

X. Investigation

Synonyms / Related Words

- Inquisitiveness
- Exploration
- Interest

IELTS Writing Task 2 – Q type : Cause and Effect Question -
Why is curiosity important in education, and what effects does it have on a student's learning process?

28. **Peace:**

Peace is a state of calm and harmony where there is no conflict, violence, or disturbance—either within individuals, communities, or nations.
10 Points You Can Use in IELTS Answers (Writing/Speaking)

1. Peace is essential for stable societies and global development.

2. It allows individuals to live without fear and pursue their goals freely.

3. Education plays a key role in promoting peace and understanding.

4. Conflict resolution skills are important to maintain peace in personal and social contexts.

5. Inner peace, or mental calmness, contributes to emotional well-being.

6. Political stability often depends on peaceful governance and fair policies.

7. Acts of kindness and empathy contribute to peaceful communities.

8. International organizations like the UN work to maintain global peace.

9. Media and cultural exchanges can foster peace through greater understanding.

10. In this world of excess information, social media interventions and stressful work and home environments peace is of high value.

10 Useful Words for IELTS Answers

I.   Harmony

II. Non-violence

III. Conflict resolution

IV. Tolerance

V.   Unity

VI. Stability

VII. Justice

VIII. Security

IX. Calmness

X. Reconciliation

Synonyms / Related Words

- Harmony
- Tranquillity
- Non-violence

IELTS Writing Task 2 – Q type : Problem–Solution Question-
Many parts of the world continue to experience conflict and violence. **What are the main causes of global unrest, and what solutions can help promote peace?**

29. **Fairness:**

Fairness is the quality of treating people equally, justly, and without favouritism or discrimination.
10 Points You Can Use in IELTS Answers (Writing/Speaking)

1. Fairness is essential in creating a just and balanced society.

2. It promotes equal opportunities regardless of background or identity.

3. In education, fairness ensures every student gets the support they need.

4. Fair treatment in the workplace leads to better morale and productivity.

5. Legal systems are built on the principle of fairness and impartial judgment.

6. Children learn fairness through social interaction and guidance from adults.

7. Unfairness can lead to resentment, social unrest, and lack of trust.

8. Fairness in sports ensures healthy competition and respect among players.

9. Governments must implement fair policies to maintain public support.

10. Fairness is closely linked to ethics, honesty, and respect for others.

10 Useful Words for IELTS Answers

I. Justice

II. Equality

III. Impartiality

IV. Honesty

V. Ethics

VI. Integrity

VII. Neutrality

VIII. Balance

IX. Equity

X. Transparency

Synonyms / Related Words

- Justice
- Impartiality
- Equity

IELTS Writing Task 2 – Q type : Agree/Disagree with Example-
Some people believe that complete fairness is impossible to achieve in society.
Do you agree or disagree with this statement? Give relevant reasons and examples from your knowledge or experience.

30. Inspiration:

Inspiration is the process of being mentally stimulated to do or feel something, especially something creative, positive, or ambitious.

10 Points You Can Use in IELTS Answers (Writing/Speaking)

1. Inspiration motivates people to set and achieve meaningful goals.

2. It can come from people, nature, art, music, or personal experiences.

3. Teachers, leaders, and role models often serve as sources of inspiration.

4. Inspirational stories can uplift individuals and boost confidence.

5. Inspiration plays a key role in creative fields like writing, painting, and music.

6. It helps individuals overcome challenges by giving them hope and direction.

7. Social media can both positively and negatively influence what inspires people.

8. Inspirational environments, such as supportive workplaces or schools, enhance productivity.

9. Inspired people are more likely to take initiative and think innovatively.

10. While inspiration is often spontaneous, it can be cultivated through habits like reading or discussions.

10 Useful Words for IELTS Answers

I. Motivation

II. Creativity

III. Influence

IV. Role model

V. Uplift

VI. Drive

VII. Determination

VIII. Empowerment

IX. Passion

X. Aspiration

Synonyms / Related Words

- Motivation
- Stimulation
- Influence

IELTS Writing Task 2 – Q type : Double Question with Example-
What inspires people to pursue their dreams?
How can someone become a source of inspiration for others?
Give relevant reasons and examples to support your answer from you knowledge or experience.

31. **Maturity:**

Maturity is the state of being fully developed in terms of behavior, emotions, and decision-making, often marked by responsibility, self-awareness, and the ability to handle situations wisely.
10 Points You Can Use in IELTS Answers (Writing/Speaking)

1. Maturity helps individuals make thoughtful and balanced decisions.

2. It is often associated with age, but emotional and mental maturity can differ widely.

3. Mature people are more likely to respond calmly under pressure.

4. Maturity involves taking responsibility for one's actions and learning from mistakes.

5. It is crucial in relationships, as it fosters understanding and compromise.

6. In the workplace, maturity enhances teamwork, leadership, and professionalism.

7. Exposure to challenges and life experiences helps build maturity.

8. Emotional maturity includes controlling impulses and being empathetic.

9. Educational systems and family upbringing play a big role in developing maturity.

10. Societies benefit when citizens show civic maturity and respect for rules.

10 Useful Words for IELTS Answers

I. Responsibility

II. Wisdom

III. Emotional intelligence

IV. Self-control

V. Rationality

VI. Decision-making

VII. Patience

VIII. Accountability

IX. Growth

X. Perspective

Synonyms / Related Words

* Wisdom
* Self-awareness
* Adulthood

IELTS Writing Task 2 – Q type : To what extent do you agree/ disagree-
People often say that maturity comes with age.
To what extent do you agree or disagree with this statement?

32. **Self-esteem:**

Self-esteem refers to a person's overall sense of self-worth or personal value—how much they respect and believe in themselves.
10 Points You Can Use in IELTS Answers (Writing/Speaking)

1. High self-esteem contributes to better mental health and emotional stability.

2. People with strong self-esteem are more confident and motivated.

3. Low self-esteem can lead to anxiety, depression, and lack of ambition.

4. Self-esteem often develops through childhood experiences and family support.

5. Positive feedback and encouragement help build self-esteem.

6. Academic and professional success can strengthen self-worth.

7. Social media can negatively affect self-esteem due to unrealistic comparisons.

8. Self-esteem affects how individuals interact with others in relationships and work.

9. Schools and workplaces can promote self-esteem by recognizing achievements.

10. Developing self-awareness and self-acceptance is key to improving self-esteem.

10 Useful Words for IELTS Answers

I. Confidence

II. Self-worth

III. Insecurity

IV. Validation

V. Motivation

VI. Acceptance

VII. Self-respect

VIII. Recognition

IX. Self-image

X. Encouragement

Synonyms / Related Words

- Self-worth
- Self-respect
- Self-image

IELTS Writing Task 2 – Q type Cause and Effect Question-
What are the main causes of low self-esteem among young people today, and how does it affect their lives?

33. **Tolerance:**

Tolerance is the willingness to accept and respect opinions, beliefs, behaviors, or practices that are different from one's own.

10 Points You Can Use in IELTS Answers (Writing/Speaking)

1. Tolerance is essential for peaceful coexistence in multicultural societies.

2. It promotes mutual respect and reduces discrimination or conflict.

3. Educational systems can foster tolerance by teaching diversity and inclusion.

4. Tolerance helps people understand and accept cultural or religious differences.

5. It plays a crucial role in maintaining harmony in globalized communities.

6. Intolerance often leads to social division, prejudice, and even violence.

7. Tolerance does not mean agreeing with everything, but respecting differences.

8. Open-minded communication is key to building a tolerant environment.

9. Leaders and public figures can influence societal levels of tolerance.

10. Tolerance is linked to emotional intelligence and empathy.

10 Useful Words for IELTS Answers

I. Respect

II. Acceptance

III. Diversity

IV. Inclusion

V.   Open-mindedness

VI.   Prejudice

VII.   Harmony

VIII.   Equality

IX.   Discrimination

X.   Understanding

Synonyms / Related Words

- Acceptance
- Open-mindedness
- Respect

IELTS Writing Task 2 – Q type Advantage–Disadvantage Outweigh Question-
Tolerance is increasingly promoted as a key value in modern society.
What are the advantages and disadvantages of encouraging tolerance?
Do you think the benefits outweigh the drawbacks?

34. **Gratitude:**

Gratitude is the quality of being thankful and showing appreciation for the kindness or help one receives from others or life in general.
10 Points You Can Use in IELTS Answers (Writing/Speaking)

1. Gratitude enhances personal happiness and well-being by fostering positive emotions.

2. Practicing gratitude can improve relationships by creating a sense of mutual appreciation.

3. Studies show that people who regularly express gratitude experience less stress and depression.

4. Gratitude encourages a mindset of abundance rather than focusing on what is lacking.

5. Acts of kindness or receiving help can inspire feelings of gratitude and appreciation.

6. Gratitude is often taught in early childhood, influencing how individuals view the world.

7. People who practice gratitude are more likely to be resilient in the face of challenges.

8. Gratitude can be expressed verbally, through gestures, or by giving back to others.

9. In work environments, gratitude helps build a positive atmosphere and improves productivity.

10. Keeping a gratitude journal is a common practice that helps individuals focus on the positive aspects of life.

10 Useful Words for IELTS Answers

I. Appreciation

II. Thankfulness

III. Acknowledgment

IV. Positivity

V. Kindness

VI. Generosity

VII. Well-being

VIII. Reflection

IX. Altruism

X. Contentment

Synonyms / Related Words

- Appreciation
- Thankfulness
- Acknowledgement

IELTS Writing Task 2 – Q type : Double Question with Example-
Why is gratitude considered an important trait in many cultures?
How can expressing gratitude can positively impact a relationship?
Give relevant reasons and examples from your knowledge or experience.

35. **Compassion:**

Compassion is the feeling of deep sympathy and concern for others who are suffering, accompanied by a desire to help alleviate their pain or difficulties.
10 Points You Can Use in IELTS Answers (Writing/Speaking)

1. Compassion leads to positive social behaviors and strengthens interpersonal relationships.

2. People with compassion are more likely to offer emotional support to others during difficult times.

3. Compassion can reduce feelings of isolation and loneliness in both the giver and receiver.

4. Many cultures emphasize compassion as an essential virtue in promoting social harmony.

5. Showing compassion towards others can improve mental health and overall well-being.

6. Compassionate acts often lead to the development of strong, empathetic communities.

7. Volunteering or helping others in need is one way to express compassion in everyday life.

8. Compassion is linked to reduced aggression and violence, contributing to peaceful societies.

9. In the workplace, compassionate leadership can enhance employee morale and productivity.

10. Practicing compassion not only helps others but can also provide the giver with a sense of purpose.

10 Useful Words for IELTS Answers

I. Empathy

II. Sympathy

III. Kindness

IV. Altruism

V. Care

VI. Generosity

VII. Support

VIII. Understanding

IX. Emotional intelligence

X. Relief

Synonyms / Related Words

- Empathy
- Sympathy
- Altruism

IELTS Writing Task 2 – Q type : Single Question-
Compassion plays an important role in creating stronger communities.
What are some ways individuals can practice compassion to help improve their communities?

36. **Patience:**

Patience is the ability to wait calmly for something without getting frustrated or upset. It involves enduring difficult situations, delays, or suffering without anger.

10 Points You Can Use in IELTS Answers (Writing/Speaking)

1. Patience is an essential skill in handling stress and frustration in everyday life.

2. Being patient allows individuals to make better decisions, as they avoid acting impulsively.

3. Patience is crucial in relationships, as it helps in resolving conflicts calmly and effectively.

4. In a fast-paced world, cultivating patience can lead to improved mental and emotional well-being.

5. People with patience are more likely to achieve long-term goals because they understand the value of persistence.

6. Patience plays a significant role in learning new skills or acquiring knowledge, especially in challenging environments.

7. It fosters a sense of resilience, enabling people to cope with adversity and setbacks.

8. Patience is necessary in the workplace, particularly in leadership roles, as it ensures thoughtful decision-making and conflict resolution.

9. Cultivating patience can reduce the risk of burnout, as individuals are less likely to feel overwhelmed by immediate demands.

10. Patience is often seen as a sign of maturity and emotional intelligence.

10 Useful Words for IELTS Answers

I. Tolerance

II. Persistence

III. Endurance

IV. Calmness

V. Resilience

VI. Composure

VII. Self-control

VIII. Forbearance

IX. Serenity

X. Temperance

Synonyms / Related Words

- Tolerance
- Endurance
- Perseverance

IELTS Writing Task 2 – Q type : Agree/Disagree Question-

Some people believe that patience is a crucial quality for success in life. **Do you agree or disagree with this opinion? Why or why not?**

37. **Integrity:**

Integrity refers to the quality of being honest, having strong moral principles, and being consistent in actions, values, and beliefs.

10 Points You Can Use in IELTS Answers (Writing/Speaking)

1. Integrity is a key element in building trust in relationships, both personal and professional.

2. People with integrity are often seen as reliable and dependable by others.

3. Integrity is crucial in leadership roles, as it helps in maintaining credibility and guiding others by example.

4. In the workplace, individuals with integrity uphold ethical standards and ensure fairness in decision-making.

5. Integrity fosters a sense of accountability, as people with integrity take responsibility for their actions.

6. A lack of integrity can lead to dishonesty, corruption, and ethical dilemmas in society.

7. Integrity contributes to long-term success, as it establishes a reputation based on trustworthiness.

8. People with integrity are less likely to be swayed by external pressures and remain true to their principles.

9. Integrity is important in academic settings, where it ensures fairness in assessments and discourages cheating.

10. Developing integrity involves practicing honesty, being transparent, and staying true to one's values, even in challenging situations.

10 Useful Words for IELTS Answers

I. Honesty

II. Trustworthiness

III. Accountability

IV. Ethics

V. Moral principles

VI. Transparency

VII. Reliability

VIII. Uprightness

IX. Sincerity

X. Fairness

Synonyms / Related Words

- Honesty
- Uprightness
- Trustworthiness

IELTS Writing Task 2 – Q type : To What Extent Do You Agree/ Disagree Question-

Integrity is often seen as one of the most important values in society.
To what extent do you agree or disagree with this statement? Give relevant reasons and examples from your knowledge or experience.

38. Mindfulness:

Mindfulness is the practice of being fully aware and present in the current moment, without judgment. It involves paying attention to thoughts, feelings, bodily sensations, and the surrounding environment with a sense of focus and calmness.

10 Points You Can Use in IELTS Answers (Writing/Speaking)

1. Mindfulness can improve mental well-being by reducing stress, anxiety, and depression.

2. It encourages self-awareness, helping individuals understand their emotions and reactions.

3. Practicing mindfulness can improve focus and concentration, leading to greater productivity.

4. It is widely used in therapy, such as Mindfulness-Based Stress Reduction (MBSR), to help manage chronic pain and other health issues.

5. Mindfulness helps in emotional regulation by fostering a balanced response to stressful situations.

6. It enhances relationships, as people become more present and empathetic with others.

7. In daily life, mindfulness encourages mindful eating, walking, and other simple activities, promoting a healthier lifestyle.

8. It supports personal growth by encouraging non-judgmental awareness of one's thoughts and actions.

9. Mindfulness techniques, such as meditation, are often used in schools and workplaces to boost mental health and performance.

10. The benefits of mindfulness extend to physical health, including lowering blood pressure and improving sleep quality.

10 Useful Words for IELTS Answers

I. Awareness

II. Meditation

III. Focus

IV. Calmness

V. Attention

VI. Clarity

VII. Present moment

VIII. Relaxation

IX. Reflection

X. Balance

Synonyms / Related Words

- Awareness
- Concentration
- Presence

IELTS Writing Task 2 – Q type : Single Opinion Question -
Some people believe that practicing mindfulness is essential for mental well-being. **Discuss the view and give your opinion. Provide examples where relevant.**

39. **Dignity:**

Dignity refers to the state of being worthy of respect and honor. It involves maintaining one's self-respect, behaving with self-worth, and treating others with a sense of respect and honor.
10 Points You Can Use in IELTS Answers (Writing/Speaking)

1. Dignity is an inherent right that every individual deserves, regardless of background, social status, or nationality.

2. Maintaining personal dignity is crucial in preserving one's sense of self-worth and confidence.

3. Dignity is a core value in human rights, as it asserts that all individuals are entitled to respect and fair treatment.

4. Upholding dignity in communication involves treating others with courtesy and listening attentively.

5. A society that respects dignity promotes equality and fairness, reducing discrimination and social injustice.

6. Many cultures place high importance on dignity, and it influences how people interact with one another.

7. Dignity can be threatened through humiliation, oppression, or degradation, which can have long-lasting emotional and psychological effects.

8. In professional settings, dignity is essential in fostering a positive and respectful work environment.

9. Personal dignity often correlates with ethical behavior and moral principles.

10. Protecting the dignity of others requires empathy and understanding, ensuring that people are treated with fairness and respect.

10 Useful Words for IELTS Answers

I. Respect

II. Honor

III. Worth

IV. Integrity

V. Equality

VI. Self-esteem

VII. Self-respect

VIII. Human rights

IX. Esteem

X. Recognition

Synonyms / Related Words

- Honour
- Respect
- Self-worth

IELTS Writing Task 2 – Q type : To what extent do you agree or disagree -

Some people believe that dignity is more important than wealth. **To what extent do you agree or disagree with this view?**

40. **Awareness:**

Awareness refers to the knowledge or understanding of a particular situation, fact, or condition. It involves being conscious of one's surroundings, emotions, and the impact of actions on others or the environment.

10 Points You Can Use in IELTS Answers (Writing/Speaking)

1. Awareness helps individuals make informed decisions, leading to better choices in life.

2. Raising awareness about social issues like climate change, poverty, and inequality is essential for creating positive change.

3. Increased awareness can foster empathy, making people more understanding and compassionate toward others.

4. Awareness is key to promoting mental health, as understanding one's emotions can lead to better emotional regulation.

5. In today's digital world, awareness about online safety is crucial to prevent cybercrime and identity theft.

6. Environmental awareness encourages people to adopt sustainable practices and protect natural resources.

7. Public health awareness campaigns can play a significant role in preventing the spread of diseases and improving community health.

8. Political awareness allows citizens to engage in the democratic process and make informed voting decisions.

9. Cultural awareness helps break down barriers between different societies and promotes inclusivity and respect.

10. Awareness of personal rights and responsibilities helps individuals navigate legal and social systems more effectively.

10 Useful Words for IELTS Answers

I. Consciousness

II. Knowledge

III. Understanding

IV. Perception

V. Recognition

VI. Realization

VII.   Sensitivity

VIII.   Mindfulness

IX.   Insight

X.   Alertness

Synonyms / Related Words

- Consciousness
- Understanding
- Insight

IELTS Writing Task 2 – Q type : Problem-Solution Question-
What are the main problems caused by a lack of awareness in society, and what can be done to address these issues?

41. Humility:

Humanity refers to the quality of being human, which includes compassion, kindness, empathy, and the ability to work together for the common good. It also refers to the collective existence of humans and the human race as a whole.

10 Points You Can Use in IELTS Answers (Writing/Speaking)

1. Humanity is about demonstrating compassion and understanding for others, especially in times of need.

2. Human beings have the ability to collaborate and build communities, showing the strength of collective efforts.

3. Humanity includes the concept of moral responsibility, where individuals help others and contribute to society.

4. The advancement of science and technology is a testament to human innovation and the betterment of life.

5. In the face of crises, humanity often comes together to provide aid, such as during natural disasters.

6. The concept of human rights is based on humanity's belief in equality, freedom, and justice for all people.

7. Humanity involves recognizing shared struggles and celebrating cultural diversity, fostering a sense of global unity.

8. As a species, humanity's progress is driven by the ability to learn, adapt, and share knowledge across generations.

9. Efforts to combat poverty, hunger, and disease demonstrate the humanitarian drive to improve the lives of others.

10. The arts and literature often reflect humanity's emotional depth, addressing both the beauty and struggles of human existence.

10 Useful Words for IELTS Answers

I. Compassion

II. Empathy

III. Altruism

IV. Cooperation

V. Solidarity

VI. Dignity

VII. Kindness

VIII. Tolerance

IX. Human rights

X. Brotherhood

Synonyms / Related Words

- Compassion
- Altruism
- Solidarity

IELTS Writing Task 2 – Q type : Advantage-Disadvantage Question-
What are the advantages and disadvantages of humanity's reliance on technology in modern society?

42. **Stress:**

Stress is a physical or emotional response to pressure, demands, or challenging situations. It can be caused by both external events (like work or exams) and internal thoughts, and it affects a person's mental and physical health.
10 Points You Can Use in IELTS Answers (Writing/Speaking)

1. Stress is a common issue in modern life, especially due to fast-paced lifestyles and work pressure.

2. It can have both positive and negative effects; for instance, mild stress can boost motivation, while chronic stress can harm health.

3. Academic pressure is a major source of stress for students, especially during exams or deadlines.

4. Workplace stress often results from long hours, unrealistic expectations, or poor management.

5. Stress can lead to health problems such as insomnia, high blood pressure, and weakened immunity.

6. Regular physical exercise, meditation, and hobbies are effective ways to manage stress.

7. Social support from friends and family plays a crucial role in reducing stress levels.

8. Technology, while helpful, can also increase stress through constant notifications and work-life imbalance.

9. Governments and companies should promote mental health awareness and provide stress-reduction programs.

10. Understanding the root causes of stress helps individuals take proactive steps toward better mental well-being.

11. 10 Vocabulary Words for the Topic:

10 Useful Words for IELTS Answers

I. Anxiety

II. Pressure

III. Burnout

IV. Overwhelmed

V. Coping

VI. Exhaustion

VII. Relaxation

VIII. Productivity

IX. Emotional well-being

X. Mindfulness

Synonyms / Related Words

- Tension
- Anxiety
- Strain

IELTS Writing Task 2 – Q type : Cause and Effect Question-
What are the main causes of stress in today's society, and what effects does it have on individuals and communities?

43. **Anxiety:**

Anxiety is a feeling of worry, nervousness, or unease about something with an uncertain outcome. It can be a temporary emotional state or a long-term mental health condition.
10 Points You Can Use in IELTS Answers (Writing/Speaking)

1. Anxiety is a common emotional response to stress, especially in high-pressure environments like school or work.

2. It can affect people's ability to focus, make decisions, and perform daily tasks effectively.

3. Academic or exam-related anxiety is especially common among students.

4. Social media has increased anxiety in many young people due to constant comparison and pressure to meet unrealistic standards.

5. While some level of anxiety is normal, chronic anxiety may require professional support or therapy.

6. Regular physical activity, mindfulness, and proper sleep are effective ways to manage anxiety.

7. Stigma around mental health can prevent individuals from seeking help for anxiety.

8. Anxiety can manifest physically through symptoms like headaches, rapid heartbeat, or stomach discomfort.

9. Employers and educational institutions should create supportive environments to reduce anxiety.

10. Raising awareness about mental health can help normalize discussions around anxiety and reduce its negative impact.

10 Useful Words for IELTS Answers

   I. Nervousness

  II. Worry

 III. Stress

 IV. Panic

  V. Pressure

 VI. Overthinking

VII. Mental health

VIII. Tension

 IX. Coping mechanisms

  X. Emotional distress

Synonyms / Related Words

- Apprehension
- Unease
- Restlessness

IELTS Writing Task 2 – Q type : Problem-Solution Question-
Many people today experience high levels of anxiety. What are the main causes of this issue, and what steps can individuals and society take to reduce it?

44. Pleasure:

Pleasure is a feeling of enjoyment, satisfaction, or happiness that comes from experiences such as hobbies, relationships, relaxation, or achievements.

10 Points You Can Use in IELTS Answers (Writing/Speaking)

1. Pleasure is an essential part of human well-being and contributes to overall life satisfaction.

2. People derive pleasure from different sources, including relationships, entertainment, travel, or nature.

3. Simple pleasures, such as a good meal or a walk in the park, can significantly improve mental health.

4. In modern life, people often struggle to find time for pleasure due to work pressure and responsibilities.

5. Excessive pursuit of pleasure, such as through unhealthy habits, can have negative long-term effects.

6. Cultural background often influences what individuals find pleasurable.

7. Leisure activities that bring pleasure can boost creativity and reduce stress.

8. Technology has changed how people experience pleasure, with digital entertainment becoming increasingly popular.

9. Emotional and physical pleasure are both important, but balance is necessary for a healthy lifestyle.

10. Governments and organizations should promote public spaces and recreational facilities to enhance societal well-being.

10 Useful Words for IELTS Answers

    I. Enjoyment

   II. Satisfaction

  III. Delight

  IV. Relaxation

   V. Happiness

  VI. Fulfillment

 VII. Gratification

VIII. Leisure

  IX. Entertainment

   X. Contentment

Synonyms / Related Words

- Enjoyment
- Delight
- Gratification

IELTS Writing Task 2 – Q type : Advantage-Disadvantage Opinion Question-

Some people believe that seeking pleasure is essential for a fulfilling life, while others think it can lead to selfishness.
What are the advantages and disadvantages of prioritizing pleasure, and what is your opinion?

45. **Pain:**

Pain is an unpleasant physical or emotional sensation that indicates injury, discomfort, or distress. It can be short-term (acute) or long-lasting (chronic), and it affects both the body and the mind.

10 Points You Can Use in IELTS Answers (Writing/Speaking)

1. Pain is a natural warning system that helps people recognize when something is wrong with their body.

2. There are two main types of pain: physical pain (e.g., injuries, illness) and emotional pain (e.g., grief, heartbreak).

3. Chronic pain can significantly reduce a person's quality of life and productivity.

4. Many people experience emotional pain due to social problems like loneliness or rejection.

5. Pain tolerance varies from person to person, often depending on mental strength and life experience.

6. Pain can be managed through medication, therapy, or natural remedies such as meditation.

7. Mental health support is essential for people suffering from emotional pain.

8. Advances in medical technology have improved pain management in hospitals and clinics.

9. People who overcome painful experiences often develop greater resilience and empathy.

10. Cultural attitudes toward pain can influence how people express or cope with it.

10 Useful Words for IELTS Answers

I. Discomfort

II. Suffering

III.   Ache

IV.   Trauma

V.   Grief

VI.   Distress

VII.   Chronic

VIII.   Relief

IX.   Tolerance

X.   Healing

Synonyms / Related Words

- Suffering
- Agony
- Discomfort

IELTS Writing Task 2 – Q type : Cause and Effect Question-
Why do people experience different types of pain, and how can pain affect their personal and professional lives?

46. **Morality:**

Morality refers to the principles or rules that guide human behavior based on ideas of what is right and wrong. It often comes from cultural, religious, or personal beliefs.

10 Points You Can Use in IELTS Answers (Writing/Speaking)

1. Morality plays a key role in shaping human behavior and decision-making.

2. It helps maintain social order by promoting fairness, respect, and justice.

3. Moral values are often taught from a young age through family, education, and religion.

4. Different cultures may have different moral standards, but some values like honesty are nearly universal.

5. In modern society, morality is increasingly influenced by media and public figures.

6. Ethical dilemmas arise when personal beliefs conflict with societal norms.

7. Schools should encourage moral education alongside academic knowledge.

8. A strong moral compass can guide individuals during difficult or unclear situations.

9. Moral behavior builds trust, which is essential in both personal and professional relationships.

10. Moral decay in society can lead to corruption, inequality, and a loss of social cohesion.

10 Useful Words for IELTS Answers

I. Ethics

II. Integrity

III. Conscience

IV. Justice

V. Virtue

VI. Honesty

VII.   Respect

VIII.   Fairness

IX.   Responsibility

X.   Values

Synonyms / Related Words

- Ethics
- Virtue
- Principles

IELTS Writing Task 2 – Q type : Agree/Disagree Question with Example-
Some people believe that morality should be taught in schools.
Do you agree or disagree? Use examples to support your view.

Common Concepts for IELTS (Core Topics)

CHAPTER II

Common Concepts

1. **Advertisement:**

Advertisement is a form of communication used to persuade people to buy products, use services, or adopt ideas. It is commonly seen in media such as TV, internet, newspapers, and billboards.

10 Points You Can Use in IELTS Answers (Writing/Speaking)

1. Advertising plays a vital role in informing consumers about new products and services.

1. It is a key strategy businesses use to increase brand awareness and boost sales.

3. Modern advertisements often use emotional appeal to connect with viewers.

4. Digital advertising, especially on social media, has become more targeted and effective.

5. Children are especially vulnerable to advertisements, which can influence their choices and behavior.

6. Some ads are misleading and create unrealistic expectations among consumers.

7. Government regulations are necessary to ensure advertisements are truthful and not harmful.

8. Celebrities and influencers are commonly used in advertisements to attract attention.

9. Repetitive advertising can lead to consumer fatigue and disinterest.

10. While advertising supports free media through funding, it can sometimes prioritize profit over ethics.

10 Useful Words for IELTS Answers

I. Consumer

II. Persuade

III. Marketing

IV. Promotion

V. Commercial

VI. Brand

VII. Influence

VIII. Strategy

IX. Audience

X. Regulation

Synonyms / Related Words

- Promotion
- Publicity
- Marketing

IELTS Writing Task 2 – Q type : Advantage-Disadvantage Outweigh Question-

Advertisements are becoming increasingly influential in our daily lives. What are the advantages and disadvantages of this trend? **Do you think the benefits outweigh the drawbacks?**

2. **Architecture:**

Architecture refers to the art and science of designing and constructing buildings and other physical structures.

10 Points You Can Use in IELTS Answers (Writing/Speaking)

1. Architecture reflects the culture and history of a society.

2. Sustainable architecture helps reduce environmental impact.

3. Modern architecture focuses on minimalism and functionality.

4. Ancient architecture often emphasized beauty and symbolism.

5. Urban areas are increasingly embracing green architecture.

6. Good architectural design can enhance quality of life.

7. Skyscrapers symbolize economic growth and technological advancement.

8. Preservation of historic architecture is essential for cultural heritage.

9. Innovative architecture can attract tourism and boost local economies.

10. Architectural styles vary widely between countries and climates.

10 Useful Words for IELTS Answers

I. Structure

II. Blueprint

III. Sustainable

IV. Aesthetic

V. Functional

VI. Urbanization

VII. Heritage

VIII. Innovation

IX. Design

X. Construction

Synonyms / Related Words

- Design
- Construction
- Structural planning

IELTS Writing Task 2 – Q type : Opinion Question with Example-
Some people believe that modern architectural designs are better suited to urban life, while others think traditional styles are more appropriate. **What are the advantages and disadvantages of each, and what is your opinion?**

3. **Art:**

Art is the expression or application of human creativity and imagination, typically in visual forms like painting, sculpture, or design, to communicate ideas or emotions.
10 Points You Can Use in IELTS Answers (Writing/Speaking)

1. Art plays a vital role in preserving cultural heritage.

2. Creative expression through art can improve mental well-being.

3. Public art enhances the aesthetic appeal of cities.

4. Art education fosters creativity and critical thinking in students.

5. Digital art has expanded accessibility to creative tools.

6. Funding for the arts supports local artists and economies.

7. Museums and galleries attract cultural tourism.

8. Art often challenges societal norms and provokes thought.

9. Traditional art forms are at risk of disappearing without support.

10. Art can be a powerful medium for social and political commentary.

10 Useful Words for IELTS Answers

I. Creativity

II. Expression

III. Visual

IV. Culture

V. Inspiration

VI. Exhibition

VII. Aesthetic

VIII. Interpretation

IX. Talent

X. Medium

Synonyms / Related Words

- Artwork
- Creative expression
- Visual art

IELTS Writing Task 2 – Q type : Cause and effect question-

Why do people create art, and what impact does it have on individuals and society

4. **Art and Society:**

Art and Society refers to the relationship between creative expression and the cultural, social, and political aspects of the communities where it exists.

10 Points You Can Use in IELTS Answers (Writing/Speaking)

1. Art reflects the values, beliefs, and issues of a society.

2. It promotes cultural awareness and social cohesion.

3. Art can challenge injustice and provoke public debate.

4. Street art and murals often address social and political themes.

5. Societies that invest in the arts tend to support innovation and free thought.

6. Art therapy is used to help people deal with trauma or mental health issues.

7. Government funding of the arts supports cultural development.

8. Art in public spaces makes culture more accessible to all.

9. Different societies interpret art through unique cultural lenses.

10. Art helps preserve history and educate future generations.

10 Useful Words for IELTS Answers

I. Culture

II. Expression

III. Social change

IV. Public awareness

V. Heritage

VI. Symbolism

VII. Engagement

VIII. Civic identity

IX. Inclusion

X. Representation

Synonyms / Related Words

- Cultural expression
- Social commentary
- Creative culture

IELTS Writing Task 2 – Q type : To what extent do you agree/disagree question-

Art is essential to the development of a healthy and progressive society. **To what extent do you agree or disagree?**

5. **Biodiversity:**

Biodiversity refers to the variety of life forms on Earth, including different species of plants, animals, fungi, and microorganisms, as well as the ecosystems they form.

10 Points You Can Use in IELTS Answers (Writing/Speaking)

1. Biodiversity is essential for maintaining ecological balance.

2. A wide variety of species supports food chains and ecosystems.

3. Loss of biodiversity can lead to the extinction of key species.

4. Human activities like deforestation and pollution threaten biodiversity.

5. Biodiverse ecosystems provide natural resources like medicine, food, and clean water.

6. Climate change is a major cause of biodiversity loss worldwide.

7. Conservation efforts aim to protect endangered species and habitats.

8. Biodiversity promotes resilience to natural disasters and environmental changes.

9. Protected areas like national parks help preserve biodiversity.

10. Education and awareness are key to encouraging biodiversity-friendly practices.

10 Useful Words for IELTS Answers

I. Ecosystem

II. Species

III. Conservation

IV. Extinction

V. Habitat

VI. Sustainability

VII. Deforestation

VIII. Climate change

IX. Pollution

X. Diversity

Synonyms / Related Words

- Biological diversity
- Natural variety
- Ecological richness

IELTS Writing Task 2 – Q type : Problem-Solution Question-
Biodiversity is declining in many parts of the world. **What are the main causes of this issue, and what solutions can be implemented.**

6. **Business:**

Business plays a crucial role in driving economic growth and providing job opportunities, shaping the livelihoods of millions globally.
10 Points You Can Use in IELTS Answers (Writing/Speaking)

1. Business plays a crucial role in economic development by creating jobs and generating wealth.

2. The rise of digital businesses and e-commerce has transformed global markets.

3. Small and medium-sized enterprises (SMEs) are vital for fostering local economies.

4. Corporate social responsibility (CSR) emphasizes the ethical obligations of businesses to contribute to societal well-being.

5. The global business environment is affected by factors like trade agreements, regulations, and technological advancements.

6. Entrepreneurship drives innovation and helps in solving societal challenges.

7. Businesses often face challenges such as competition, market demand, and resource management.

8. The rise of remote work and online businesses has changed the traditional business landscape.

9. Effective leadership and management are key to the success of any business.

10. The impact of business on the environment is growing, leading to more focus on sustainable business practices.

10 Useful Words for IELTS Answers

   I. Entrepreneurship

  II. Profit

 III. E-commerce

 IV. Innovation

  V. Sustainability

 VI. Competition

VII. Market demand

VIII. Corporate responsibility

 IX. Globalization

  X. Leadership

Synonyms / Related Words

- Enterprise
- Company
- Corporation

IELTS Writing Task 2 – Q type : Advantage-Disadvantage Outweigh Question-

Do the advantages of running a business outweigh the disadvantages? Provide reasons and examples to support your answer

.

7. **Capital Punishment:**

Capital punishment refers to the legal process where a person is sentenced to death by the state as a punishment for a crime, typically serious offenses like murder or terrorism.

10 Points You Can Use in IELTS Answers (Writing/Speaking)

1. Capital punishment is a controversial issue debated worldwide for its morality and effectiveness.

2. It is often used as a deterrent for serious crimes such as murder, terrorism, and drug trafficking.

3. Some believe it delivers justice and closure to victims' families.

4. Opponents argue it is inhumane and violates human rights.

5. There is a risk of executing innocent people due to judicial errors.

6. Life imprisonment can be an effective and reversible alternative.

7. The death penalty is abolished in many countries but still practiced in others.

8. It can be disproportionately applied to minorities or the poor.

9. Studies are inconclusive on whether capital punishment deters crime.

10. Public opinion on the death penalty varies greatly by country, culture, and crime rates.

10 Useful Words for IELTS Answers

I.   Execution

II.   Deterrent

III.   Retribution

IV.   Judicial system

V.   Life imprisonment

VI.   Clemency

VII.   Morality

VIII.   Human rights

IX.   Wrongful conviction

X.   Rehabilitation

Synonyms / Related Words

- Death penalty
- State execution
- Judicial killing

IELTS Writing Task 2 – Q type : Advantage–Disadvantage Opinion Question-

Capital punishment is used in some countries as a way to deal with serious crimes. **What are the advantages and disadvantages of this practice, and do you think it is a justified form of punishment?.**

8. **City Life:**

City life refers to the lifestyle, experiences, and daily activities of people living in urban areas, typically marked by faster pace, diverse opportunities, and advanced infrastructure.

10 Points You Can Use in IELTS Answers (Writing/Speaking)

1. City life offers better access to education, healthcare, and job opportunities.

2. Urban areas are usually well-connected with public transportation.

3. Cities provide a wider range of entertainment and cultural activities.

4. High population density can lead to overcrowding and noise pollution.

5. The cost of living in cities is often higher than in rural areas.

6. Air and water pollution are common environmental problems in cities.

7. Urban residents may experience more stress due to fast-paced lifestyles.

8. Cities attract people from different backgrounds, promoting cultural diversity.

9. Technological infrastructure in cities often enhances convenience.

10. Green spaces and smart urban planning can improve city living conditions.

10 Useful Words for IELTS Answers

I. Urban

II. Infrastructure

III. Commuting

IV. Overcrowding

V. Amenities

VI. Pollution

VII. Lifestyle

VIII. Opportunity

  IX. Diversity

   X. Cost of living

Synonyms / Related Words

- Urban lifestyle
- Metropolitan living
- Urban environment

IELTS Writing Task 2 – Q type : Advantage-Disadvantage Outweigh Question-

Living in a city has both advantages and disadvantages. **Do the advantages of city life outweigh the disadvantages?**

9. **Climate Change:**

Climate change refers to significant and long-term changes in temperature, weather patterns, and other climatic conditions on Earth. It is primarily driven by human activities, such as deforestation, industrialization, and the burning of fossil fuels, which release greenhouse gases and lead to global warming.

10 Points You Can Use in IELTS Answers (Writing/Speaking)

1. Climate change is causing more frequent and severe weather events, such as hurricanes, droughts, and floods.

2. Rising global temperatures are melting polar ice caps and causing sea levels to rise, threatening coastal communities.

3. Greenhouse gases like carbon dioxide and methane are the leading contributors to global warming.

4. Human activities, including deforestation and industrial pollution, have accelerated the pace of climate change.

5. The agricultural sector is heavily affected by climate change, with altered rainfall patterns impacting food production.

6. Governments and international organizations are pushing for policy changes to reduce carbon emissions and mitigate climate change.

7. Renewable energy sources, such as solar and wind power, offer potential solutions to reduce reliance on fossil fuels.

8. Climate change disproportionately affects vulnerable populations, including low-income communities and small island nations.

9. Public awareness and education about climate change are crucial in encouraging individuals and businesses to take action.

10. Climate change presents both environmental and economic challenges, as the costs of disaster recovery and adaptation are increasing.

10 Useful Words for IELTS Answers

I. Greenhouse gases

II. Global warming

III. Emissions

IV. Sustainability

V. Renewable energy

VI. Carbon footprint

VII. Environmental degradation

VIII. Fossil fuels

IX. Adaptation

X. Mitigation

Synonyms / Related Words

- Global warming
- Environmental change
- Carbon emissions

IELTS Writing Task 2 – Q type : Cause and Effect Question-
What are the main causes of climate change, and what effects is it having on the environment?

10. **Commuication:**

Communication is vital in both personal and professional settings, influencing relationships, decision-making, and the functioning of society.
10 Points You Can Use in IELTS Answers (Writing/Speaking)

1. Effective communication is essential for building strong relationships and avoiding misunderstandings.

2. Technology has transformed communication, making it faster and more accessible through tools like email, social media, and video calls.

3. Non-verbal communication, such as body language and facial expressions, plays a crucial role in understanding messages.

4. In the workplace, clear communication improves productivity and collaboration between teams.

5. Miscommunication can lead to conflict, confusion, and inefficiency in both personal and professional environments.

6. Different cultures have varied communication styles, which can influence how messages are interpreted.

7. The rise of digital communication has reduced face-to-face interactions, potentially weakening interpersonal skills.

8. Active listening is an important part of effective communication, ensuring that the listener fully understands the speaker's message.

9. Communication barriers, such as language differences or poor technology infrastructure, can hinder effective interaction.

10. Emotional intelligence enhances communication by allowing individuals to navigate sensitive topics with empathy and understanding.

10 Useful Words for IELTS Answers

   I. Verbal communication

  II. Non-verbal communication

 III. Dialogue

 IV. Interaction

  V. Misunderstanding

 VI. Empathy

 VII. Body language

VIII. Active listening

 IX. Expression

  X. Digital communication

Synonyms / Related Words

- Conversation
- Discussion
- Correspondence (for written communication)

IELTS Writing Task 2 – Q type : Single Opinion Question with Example-

Some people believe that face-to-face communication is better than digital communication.

Discuss your views and give your opinion. Give relevant reasons and examples from your knowledge or experience.

11. Computers:

Computers have an integral part of our day- to day life. The world has progressed so much that even the simplest of actions are reliant of computers for simplicity and precision.

10 Points You Can Use in IELTS Answers (Writing/Speaking)

1. Computers are widely used in education for online learning and research.
2. They improve productivity in workplaces through automation and data management.

3. The internet, powered by computers, connects people globally.

4. Many jobs now require computer literacy and digital skills.

5. Computers enable remote work and virtual collaboration.

6. Overuse of computers can lead to physical and mental health issues.

7. Cybercrime and hacking are increasing with greater computer use.

8. They support medical research, diagnostics, and patient records.

9. AI and machine learning depend on computer technology.

10. Children benefit from educational games but may become overly dependent on screens.

10 Useful Words for IELTS Answers

I. Digital

II. Automation

III. Connectivity

IV. Efficiency

V. Innovation

VI. Virtual

VII. Cybersecurity

VIII. Programming

IX. Screen time

X. Data processing

Synonyms / Related Words

- Digital devices
- Electronic machines
- Information technology tools

IELTS Writing Task 2 – Q type : Agree/Disagree with Example-
Some people believe that computers make people less productive. **Do you agree or disagree? Include examples to support your opinion.**

12. **Conservation:**

Conservation is the protection, preservation, and careful management of the natural environment, wildlife, and resources to prevent degradation and ensure sustainability for future generations.

10 Points You Can Use in IELTS Answers (Writing/Speaking)

1. Conservation helps maintain biodiversity and ecological balance.

2. Natural resources like water, forests, and fossil fuels need to be conserved.

3. Wildlife conservation prevents species extinction.

4. Governments and NGOs run campaigns to raise awareness about conservation.

5. Conservation efforts are vital in combating climate change.

6. Protected areas such as national parks help preserve ecosystems.

7. Overconsumption and industrialization threaten conservation goals.

8. Education plays a key role in promoting conservation-friendly behavior.

9. Renewable energy supports conservation by reducing pollution.

10. Local communities can actively participate in conservation programs.

10 Useful Words for IELTS Answers

I. Sustainability

II. Ecosystem

III. Biodiversity

IV. Preservation

V. Endangered

VI. Natural resources

VII. Deforestation

VIII. Pollution

  IX. Awareness

   X. Habitat

Synonyms / Related Words

- Preservation
- Environmental protection
- Resource management

IELTS Writing Task 2 – Q type : Double Question-
Why is conservation important in today's world? What actions can individuals take to contribute to environmental conservation?

13. **Consumerism:**

Consumerism encourages constant purchasing as a path to happiness, often leading to overconsumption and environmental strain. It can blur the line between wants and needs, shaping identities through material possessions.

10 Points You Can Use in IELTS Answers (Writing/Speaking)

1. Consumerism drives economic growth by encouraging spending.

2. It often leads to overproduction and environmental degradation.

3. Advertising plays a major role in promoting consumerist habits.

4. Many people associate material possessions with success or happiness.

5. Consumerism can result in waste, pollution, and resource depletion.

6. It contributes to the rise of fast fashion and planned obsolescence.

7. Ethical concerns are growing about how products are sourced and made.

8. Minimalism and sustainable living are responses to excessive consumerism.

9. Consumerism impacts mental health through pressure to constantly buy.

10. Governments and educators can promote awareness of responsible consumption.

10 Useful Words for IELTS Answers

I. Materialism

II. Sustainability

III. Waste

IV. Consumption

V. Advertising

VI. Overproduction

VII. Minimalism

VIII. Excess

IX. Economy

X. Lifestyle

Synonyms / Related Words

- Materialism
- Consumption culture
- Commercialism

IELTS Writing Task 2 – Q type : Advantage-Disadvantage Opinion Question-

Some people think consumerism improves the economy, while others believe it harms society and the environment. **What are the advantages and disadvantages of consumerism, and what is your opinion?**

14. **Culture:**

Culture shapes how people interact, express themselves, and view the world, playing a vital role in identity and community life.

10 Points You Can Use in IELTS Answers (Writing/Speaking)

1. Culture reflects a society's history, traditions, and values.

2. Globalization has both enriched and threatened local cultures.

3. Cultural exchange promotes understanding and reduces prejudice between nations.

4. Language is a key component of culture and often defines a group's identity.

5. Traditional customs and festivals are important for preserving cultural heritage.

6. Cultural diversity contributes to a richer, more inclusive society.

7. Media and the internet influence and sometimes homogenize global culture.

8. Cultural misunderstandings can cause conflict in international communication.

9. Governments and educational systems play a role in protecting and promoting cultural traditions.

10. Tourism can help preserve culture but may also lead to commercialization of cultural practices.

10 Useful Words for IELTS Answers

I. Heritage

II. Tradition

III. Diversity

IV. Identity

V. Globalization

VI. Customs

VII. Ethnicity

VIII. Cultural preservation

IX. Multiculturalism

X. Indigenous

Synonyms / Related Words

- Tradition
- Heritage
- Way of life

IELTS Writing Task 2 – Q type : Advantage–Disadvantage Outweigh Question-

Some people believe that globalization is leading to the disappearance of traditional cultures. **Do the advantages of globalization outweigh the disadvantages in this context?**

15. **Crime and Punishment:**

Crime and punishment are deeply intertwined concepts that reflect the moral and societal consequences of actions. The idea suggests that committing a crime inevitably leads to some form of punishment, whether it's legal, psychological, or emotional, highlighting the struggle between guilt and justice.

10 Points You Can Use in IELTS Answers (Writing/Speaking)

1. Crime rates are often influenced by social, economic, and cultural factors.

2. The justice system aims to provide fair punishment to offenders, preventing further crimes.

3. Rehabilitation is an important aspect of modern punishment to reintegrate criminals into society.

4. Some argue that the death penalty is an outdated and inhumane form of punishment.

5. Crime prevention strategies focus on addressing the root causes of criminal behavior.

6. In some countries, prison overcrowding is a serious issue due to high crime rates.

7. Punishment should be proportionate to the severity of the crime committed.

8. Crime can be reduced through better education, employment opportunities, and community engagement.

9. Technological advancements, such as surveillance cameras, are often used to deter crime.

10. The effectiveness of punitive measures versus rehabilitative programs remains a topic of debate.

10 Useful Words for IELTS Answers

I. Justice

II. Punishment

III.   Rehabilitation

IV.   Crime rate

 V.   Offender

VI.   Deterrent

VII.   Legal system

VIII.   Recidivism

IX.   Sentence

 X.   Penalties

Synonyms / Related Words

- Criminal justice
- Legal consequences
- Offense and retribution

IELTS Writing Task 2 – Q type : Agree/Disagree with Example-
Some people believe that harsh punishments are the most effective way to reduce crime, while others argue that rehabilitation programs are more beneficial. **Do you agree or disagree with this statement? Include examples to support your opinion.**

16. **Deforestation:**

Deforestation refers to the large-scale clearing or removal of forests, often to make way for agriculture, urbanization, or logging, leading to significant environmental and ecological impacts.
10 Points You Can Use in IELTS Answers (Writing/Speaking)

1. Deforestation contributes to loss of biodiversity by destroying animal habitats.

2. The clearing of forests leads to increased greenhouse gas emissions, contributing to climate change.

3. Agricultural expansion, particularly for crops like palm oil and soy, is a primary cause of deforestation.

4. Logging for timber and paper products is a major driver of forest destruction.

5. Forests play a crucial role in regulating water cycles and preventing soil erosion.

6. Reforestation and afforestation efforts are essential for mitigating deforestation impacts.

7. Illegal logging and poor enforcement of environmental laws exacerbate deforestation.

8. Deforestation threatens indigenous communities that rely on forests for their livelihoods.

9. Urbanization and infrastructure development are leading causes of forest loss in some regions.

10. Consumer demand for products like beef, coffee, and paper contribute to deforestation.

10 Useful Words for IELTS Answers

I. Biodiversity

II. Ecosystem

III. Carbon footprint

IV. Habitat

V. Reforestation

VI. Conservation

VII. Deforestation rate

VIII. Sustainability

IX. Greenhouse gases

X. Soil erosion

Synonyms / Related Words

- Forest destruction
- Tree cutting
- Land clearing

IELTS Writing Task 2 – Q type : Problem-Solution Question-
What are the main causes of deforestation, and what can be done to prevent it?

17. **Development:**

Development refers to the process of growth and improvement in a country's economic, social, and technological aspects. It often includes advancements in infrastructure, education, healthcare, and living standards, contributing to overall societal progress.

10 Points You Can Use in IELTS Answers (Writing/Speaking)

1. Economic development is essential for improving quality of life and reducing poverty.

2. Sustainable development balances economic growth with environmental protection.

3. Education and innovation play a central role in long-term development.

4. Urban development often brings job opportunities but can also lead to overcrowding and pollution.

5. Developing countries face unique challenges like limited resources and inadequate infrastructure.

6. Foreign investment and international aid can support development in poorer regions.

7. Technological development boosts productivity and global competitiveness.

8. Social development ensures equal access to healthcare, education, and opportunities.

9. Infrastructure development (roads, electricity, water supply) is fundamental for economic progress.

10. Rapid development without regulation can result in environmental degradation and social inequality.

10 Useful Words for IELTS Answers

I. Infrastructure

II. Sustainability

III. Innovation

IV. Progress

V. Urbanization

VI. Industrialization

VII. Investment

VIII. Poverty reduction

IX. Growth

X. Modernization

Synonyms / Related Words

- Progress
- Advancement
- Growth

IELTS Writing Task 2 – Q type : Cause and Effect Question-
What are the main causes of uneven development among countries, and how does it affect global stability?

18. **Economy:**

Economy refers to the system by which goods and services are produced, distributed, and consumed within a country or region. It includes factors like employment, income, trade, industry, and government policies that influence overall financial stability and growth.

10 Points You Can Use in IELTS Answers (Writing/Speaking)

1. A strong economy leads to higher employment rates, better wages, and improved living standards.

2. Economic growth is essential for national development and reducing poverty.

3. Governments use monetary and fiscal policies to manage economic stability.

4. Globalization has connected economies worldwide, boosting trade but also creating dependency.

5. Unemployment and inflation are common indicators of economic problems.

6. Small businesses and entrepreneurship play a vital role in economic development.

7. Economic inequality remains a major challenge in both developed and developing nations.

8. The informal economy contributes to national income but is often unregulated.

9. Investment in infrastructure and education can stimulate economic growth.

10. The rise of the digital economy has transformed job markets and business models.

10 Useful Words for IELTS Answers

I. Inflation

II. GDP (Gross Domestic Product)

III. Recession

IV. Employment

V. Investment

VI. Trade

VII. Economic growth

VIII. Income inequality

IX. Market

X. Financial stability

Synonyms / Related Words

- Financial system
- Economic structure

- National income

IELTS Writing Task 2 – Q type : Advantage–Disadvantage Opinion Question-
Some people believe that a growing economy benefits everyone in society. **What are the advantages and disadvantages of economic growth, and state your opinion.**

19. **Education:**

Education, the process of acquiring knowledge, skills, values, and attitudes through learning in schools, universities, or other settings, plays a critical role in personal development, social mobility, and the advancement of society as a whole.
10 Points You Can Use in IELTS Answers (Writing/Speaking)

1. Education is fundamental to both individual success and national development.

2. Equal access to quality education remains a global challenge, especially in developing countries.

3. Formal education helps develop critical thinking and problem-solving skills.

4. Online learning has transformed the traditional education system, offering flexibility and accessibility.

5. The role of teachers is vital in shaping students' academic and moral development.

6. Higher education increases job opportunities and earning potential.

7. Some argue that practical skills should be prioritized over theoretical knowledge.

8. Education systems vary globally in terms of curriculum, assessment, and teaching methods.

9. Lifelong learning is increasingly important in a fast-changing, knowledge-based economy.

10. Governments often invest in education to reduce poverty and improve social equity.

10 Useful Words for IELTS Answers

I. Curriculum

II. Literacy

III. Higher education

IV. E-learning

V. Academic performance

VI. Scholarship

VII. Tuition fees

VIII. Vocational training

IX. Knowledge acquisition

X. Educational inequality

Synonyms / Related Words

- Learning
- Schooling
- Academic instruction

IELTS Writing Task 2 – Q type : Agree/Disagree with Example-
Some people believe that academic subjects such as mathematics and science should be prioritized over music and art in schools. **Do you agree or disagree? Provide examples to support your view.**

20. **Environment:**

The environment refers to the natural world around us, including air, water, land, animals, and ecosystems. It is essential for human survival and well-being, but is increasingly threatened by pollution, climate change, deforestation, and other human activities.

10 Points You Can Use in IELTS Answers (Writing/Speaking)

1. Environmental protection is vital to ensuring the planet remains habitable for future generations.

2. Pollution of air, water, and soil has become a global crisis, especially in urban areas.

3. Climate change is a major environmental issue driven by greenhouse gas emissions.

4. Deforestation contributes to biodiversity loss and worsens global warming.

5. Renewable energy sources like solar and wind are essential for a sustainable future.

6. Governments and individuals both play a role in protecting the environment.

7. Environmental education can raise awareness and promote responsible behavior.

8. Recycling and waste management help reduce environmental damage.

9. Industrialization often leads to environmental degradation if not properly regulated.

10. International cooperation is necessary to address global environmental challenges.

10 Useful Words for IELTS Answers

I. Sustainability

II. Pollution

III. Conservation

IV. Biodiversity

V. Deforestation

VI. Emissions

VII. Climate change

VIII. Renewable energy

IX. Ecosystem

X. Greenhouse gases

Synonyms / Related Words

- Natural world
- Ecology
- Biosphere

IELTS Writing Task 2 – Q type : Problem–Solution Question-
Environmental problems are becoming a serious concern in many parts of the world. **What are the main causes of these issues, and what solutions can be implemented to address them?**

21. **Entertainment:**

Entertainment refers to activities, performances, or content designed to amuse, engage, or relax people, including music, movies, sports, gaming, and live shows. It plays an important role in modern life by providing stress relief, social interaction, and cultural expression.
10 Points You Can Use in IELTS Answers (Writing/Speaking)

1. Entertainment is essential for mental relaxation and stress reduction in today's fast-paced world.

2. Digital platforms like streaming services have revolutionized the way people consume entertainment.

3. The entertainment industry significantly contributes to the global economy through jobs and revenue.

4. Excessive consumption of entertainment, especially through screens, can lead to addiction or social isolation.

5. Traditional forms of entertainment such as theater and live music remain culturally significant.

6. Entertainment can be educational, such as documentaries or historical films.

7. Globalization has led to the international spread of entertainment content, influencing local cultures.

8. Children are highly influenced by the media they consume, raising concerns about age-appropriate content.

9. Social media has blurred the line between entertainment and real life, changing how people interact.

10. Governments often regulate entertainment content to align with cultural and moral values.

10 Useful Words for IELTS Answers

I. Leisure

II. Recreation

III. Media

   IV.   Streaming

    V.   Audience

   VI.   Popular culture

  VII.   Content

 VIII.   Addiction

   IX.   Broadcast

    X.   Performance

Synonyms / Related Words

- Leisure activities
- Recreation
- Amusement

IELTS Writing Task 2 – Q type : Opinion Question with Example-
Some people believe that entertainment hold high value in our daily lives whereas there are others who hold that it is not as essential as many of our basic needs

Discuss both views and give your opinion. Provide examples where relevant.

22. **Family:**

Family is the foundation of society and plays a central role in shaping values, identity, and behavior.
10 Points You Can Use in IELTS Answers (Writing/Speaking)

1. The family unit is essential for a child's upbringing and emotional development.

2. Modern families are more diverse, including single-parent households, same-sex parents, and blended families.

3. The traditional extended family model is becoming less common due to urbanization and mobility.

4. Technology affects how families interact, sometimes enhancing communication and sometimes reducing quality time.

5. Parents are primary role models and influence a child's habits, education, and social behavior.

6. Family support is vital during life transitions, such as illness, job loss, or major decisions.

7. Work-life balance is a growing concern, as long working hours reduce family interaction.

8. In some cultures, family obligations outweigh individual goals, especially regarding marriage and career.

9. Elderly care is often a family responsibility, but this is shifting with changing social norms.

10. Conflicts within families, if unresolved, can have long-term emotional and psychological consequences.

10 Useful Words for IELTS Answers

I. Upbringing

II. Bond

III. Parenthood

IV. Household

V. Kinship

VI. Generation gap

VII.   Support system

VIII. Family dynamics

IX.   Sibling

X.   Dependency

Synonyms / Related Words

- Household
- Relatives
- Kin

IELTS Writing Task 2 – Q type : Double Question with Example-
What role does the family play in a person's life, and how has this role changed over the past few decades? **Give relevant reasons and examples from your knowledge or experience.**

23. **Food and Nutrition:**

Food and nutrition are essential for maintaining health, supporting growth, and fuelling the body's daily activities. A balanced diet rich in vitamins, minerals, proteins, fats, and carbohydrates helps prevent disease and promotes overall well-being.
10 Points You Can Use in IELTS Answers (Writing/Speaking)

1. A nutritious diet is essential for maintaining both physical and mental health.
2. Many modern diets are high in sugar and fat but lack essential nutrients.
3. Governments can promote healthy eating through public awareness campaigns.
4. School lunches should include more fruits and vegetables to encourage healthy habits.
5. The rise of fast food culture has led to an increase in obesity and lifestyle diseases.
6. Cooking at home allows people to control ingredients and portions more effectively.

7. Income and education often influence people's ability to access nutritious food.
8. Food labeling can help consumers make more informed dietary choices.
9. Globalization has diversified diets but also led to a loss of traditional eating patterns.
10. Sustainable food systems are crucial to both human health and environmental protection.

10 Useful Words for IELTS Answers

    I. Nutrient
   II. Dietary
  III. Obesity
  IV. Processed
   V. Organic
  VI. Moderation
 VII. Malnutrition
VIII. Well-being
  IX. Consumption
   X. Metabolism

Synonyms / Related Words

- Nutrition
- Food
- Healthy eating

IELTS Writing Task 2 – Q type : Cause and Effect Question-
What are the causes of poor nutrition in modern societies, and what effects does it have on individuals and public health?

24. **Gender Issues:**

Gender issues refer to the inequalities, stereotypes, and social roles assigned based on one's gender, often leading to discrimination and limited opportunities. Addressing gender issues is essential for promoting equality, justice, and balanced development in any society.

10 Points You Can Use in IELTS Answers (Writing/Speaking)

1. Gender equality is fundamental to creating inclusive and fair societies.

2. Women still face significant barriers in employment, leadership, and education.

3. Stereotypes about gender roles begin early and are often reinforced by media and culture.

4. Equal pay for equal work remains a major concern in many parts of the world.

5. Men also face gender-related challenges, particularly regarding emotional expression and parental rights.

6. Education can play a key role in breaking gender biases from a young age.

7. Legal reforms are needed to protect people from gender-based violence and discrimination.

8. Social attitudes often lag behind laws when it comes to true gender equality.

9. Workplaces benefit from gender diversity, leading to better decision-making and innovation.

10. Promoting gender equity helps reduce poverty and improve overall human development.

10 Useful Words for IELTS Answers

I. Equality

II. Discrimination

III. Stereotypes

IV. Bias

   V. Inclusion

  VI. Empowerment

 VII. Prejudice

VIII. Representation

  IX. Equity

   X. Patriarchy

Synonyms / Related Words

- Gender Issues
- Equality
- Discrimination

IELTS Writing Task 2 – Q type : Advantage-Disadvantage Question-
What are the advantages and disadvantages of promoting gender equality in the workplace?

25. Globalization:

Globalization refers to the growing interconnectedness of the world through trade, technology, culture, and communication. While it offers economic growth and cultural exchange, it also raises concerns about inequality, cultural erosion, and environmental impact.

10 Points You Can Use in IELTS Answers (Writing/Speaking)

1. Globalization allows countries to access a wider variety of goods and services.

2. It encourages the free flow of information, ideas, and innovations across borders.

3. Multinational corporations benefit from globalization by expanding their markets.

4. Globalization has led to job creation in developing countries, but often with low wages.

5. Cultural diversity is promoted through global communication and travel.

6. Local cultures and languages may be at risk due to the dominance of global media.

7. Environmental degradation can increase due to mass production and overconsumption.

8. Global supply chains can make economies more vulnerable to international crises.

9. Education systems worldwide are becoming more aligned through global standards.

10. It can widen the gap between rich and poor nations if not managed fairly.

10 Useful Words for IELTS Answers

I. Interconnectedness

II. Multinational

III. Cultural exchange

IV. Outsourcing

V. Inequality

VI. Integration

VII. Homogenization

VIII. Trade liberalization

IX. Mobility

X. Sovereignty

Synonyms / Related Words

- International Integration
- Global Economy
- Cultural Spread

IELTS Writing Task 2 – Q type : Agree/Disagree with Example-
Some people believe that globalization is beneficial for all countries, while others think it has negative impacts. **Do you agree or disagree? Give reasons and examples.**

26. **Global Issues:**

Global issues such as climate change, poverty, and political instability affect nations across borders and require collective action. These problems pose serious threats to environmental sustainability, economic growth, and human welfare.
10 Points You Can Use in IELTS Answers (Writing/Speaking)

1. Climate change is one of the most pressing global challenges, causing rising sea levels and extreme weather.

2. Global poverty continues to affect millions, limiting access to food, education, and healthcare.

3. Political conflicts and wars result in refugee crises and disrupt global peace.

4. Pollution, especially plastic and air pollution, contributes to health issues and environmental degradation.

5. Overpopulation puts pressure on natural resources and public services.

6. Economic inequality between nations creates tension and hinders global development.

7. Global pandemics, like COVID-19, highlight the need for international cooperation in healthcare.

8. Deforestation and loss of biodiversity threaten ecosystems and climate stability.

9. Technological advancements, while beneficial, also lead to issues like cybersecurity threats and job displacement.

10. International cooperation through organizations like the UN is essential to effectively tackle global issues.

10 Useful Words for IELTS Answers

I. Sustainability

II. Inequality

III. Conflict

IV. Cooperation

V. Environment

VI. Development

VII. Crisis

VIII. Resources

IX. Globalization

X. Emissions

Synonyms / Related Words

- Worldwide challenges
- International concerns

- Cross-border problems

IELTS Writing Task 2 – Q type : Problem-Solution Question-
What are the main problems associated with global issues today, and how can they be effectively addressed?

27. **Government and Society:**

The relationship between government and society plays a crucial role in shaping the quality of life and ensuring social order. Effective governance helps maintain justice, security, and development while addressing the needs of diverse communities.

10 Points You Can Use in IELTS Answers (Writing/Speaking)

1. Governments are responsible for creating laws that maintain peace and protect citizens' rights.

2. Public services such as healthcare, education, and infrastructure are largely managed and funded by the state.

3. Transparency and accountability in government strengthen public trust and societal cohesion.

4. In democratic societies, citizens participate in governance through voting and civic engagement.

5. Corruption and misuse of power can weaken institutions and lead to social unrest.

6. Social welfare programs help reduce inequality and support vulnerable populations.

7. Governments often balance individual freedoms with national security to protect society.

8. Public policies on taxation, housing, and employment directly influence social development.

9. Collaboration between government and non-governmental organizations can improve service delivery.

10. Informed and educated citizens are essential for a healthy democracy and responsive government.

10 Useful Words for IELTS Answers

I. Legislation

II. Democracy

III. Accountability

IV. Welfare

V. Corruption

VI. Authority

VII. Infrastructure

VIII. Policy

IX. Governance

X. Citizenship

Synonyms / Related Words

- Administration
- Ruling Body
- Public management

IELTS Writing Task 2 – Q type : Opinion Question with Example-
There are people who believe that governments should be responsible for ensuring good eating habits in people and others argue that it is solely a pcrson's own responsibility.

Discuss both views and give your opinion. Give relevant reasons and examples from your knowledge or experience.

28. **Habits like reading exercise and hobbies:**

Positive habits such as reading, regular exercise, and engaging in hobbies contribute significantly to mental and physical well-being. These activities not only reduce stress but also improve focus, creativity, and overall quality of life.

10 Points You Can Use in IELTS Answers (Writing/Speaking)

1. Reading enhances vocabulary, comprehension, and critical thinking skills.

2. Regular exercise improves physical health, boosts energy, and helps prevent chronic illnesses.

3. Hobbies like painting or gardening foster creativity and reduce anxiety.

4. Developing good habits from a young age leads to long-term benefits in adulthood.

5. These activities can offer a productive break from digital screens and social media.

6. Group hobbies or fitness routines encourage social interaction and build community.

7. Time spent on meaningful activities increases overall happiness and life satisfaction.

8. Good habits can improve time management and self-discipline.

9. Engaging in leisure activities is important for maintaining a healthy work-life balance.

10. People with regular positive habits often report better sleep and mental clarity.

10 Useful Words for IELTS Answers

I. Routine

II. Discipline

III. Productivity

IV. Mindfulness

V. Creativity

VI. Relaxation

VII. Consistency

VIII. Motivation

IX. Leisure

X. Wellness

Synonyms / Related Words

- Routines
- Interests
- Practices

IELTS Writing Task 2 – Q type : Single Opinion Question with Example-
Do you think habits like reading and exercise are essential for a balanced life? **Give reasons for your answer and include any relevant examples.**

29. **Health:**

Health is a fundamental aspect of human life that affects one's ability to work, learn, and enjoy daily activities. Maintaining good health requires a balanced lifestyle, including proper nutrition, exercise, and mental well-being.

10 Points You Can Use in IELTS Answers (Writing/Speaking)

1. A healthy diet plays a crucial role in preventing lifestyle-related diseases.

2. Regular physical activity boosts immunity and cardiovascular health.

3. Mental health is as important as physical health and needs equal attention.

4. Governments should invest in public healthcare systems to ensure access for all.

5. Health education can help people make informed lifestyle choices.

6. Smoking, excessive drinking, and poor diet are major causes of preventable diseases.

7. Technology has improved healthcare but also contributed to sedentary lifestyles.

8. Stress management is essential for maintaining overall wellness.

9. Preventive care is more cost-effective than treating diseases later.

10. A healthy population contributes positively to a nation's productivity and economy.

10 Useful Words for IELTS Answers

I. Well-being

II. Nutrition

III. Fitness

IV. Prevention

V. Treatment

VI. Lifestyle

VII. Immunity

VIII. Hygiene

IX. Healthcare

X. Diagnosis

Synonyms / Related Words

- Well being
- Wellness
- Fitness

IELTS Writing Task 2 – Q type : Cause and Effect Question-
What are the main causes of poor health in modern society, and what effects do they have on individuals and communities?

30. **Internet:**

The internet has revolutionized modern life, transforming how people communicate, learn, and work. While it offers immense convenience and access to information, it also raises concerns about privacy, addiction, and misinformation.
10 Points You Can Use in IELTS Answers (Writing/Speaking)

1. The internet provides instant access to vast information, enhancing education and research.

2. Online platforms have made global communication and social interaction easier than ever.

3. E-commerce and remote work have flourished due to internet advancements.

4. Excessive internet use can lead to mental health issues and reduced productivity.

5. The internet exposes users to risks like cyberbullying, data theft, and identity fraud.

6. Students can access free online courses and educational resources globally.

7. Social media can influence opinions and spread both positive messages and false information.

8. Internet access is a key factor in the digital divide between developed and developing regions.

9. Online banking and digital services improve convenience but also pose cybersecurity risks.

10. Governments and companies must ensure responsible internet use through regulations and awareness campaigns.

10 Useful Words for IELTS Answers

I. Connectivity

II. Digital

III. Cybersecurity

IV. Communication

V. Misinformation

VI. Accessibility

VII. Privacy

VIII. E-learning

IX.   Streaming

X.   Innovation

Synonyms / Related Words

- Cyber space
- Digital world
- Virtual

IELTS Writing Task 2 – Q type : Agree/Disagree with Example-
Some people believe the internet has done more harm than good. **Do you agree or disagree? Give reasons for your answer and include examples from your own experience.**

31.   **Job:**

A job is not only a means of earning income but also a way to gain identity, purpose, and social status. In today's competitive world, job satisfaction and work-life balance are becoming increasingly important for personal well-being.
10 Points You Can Use in IELTS Answers (Writing/Speaking)

1. Employment provides financial stability and supports an individual's basic needs.

2. Job satisfaction is linked to productivity and overall happiness.

3. Many people today prefer flexible work options like remote jobs and freelancing.

4. High unemployment rates can lead to economic instability and social issues.

5. Career growth and training opportunities are key factors when choosing a job.

6. Some jobs carry more social respect and responsibility than others.

7. Technological advancement is rapidly changing the job market.

8. Work-related stress can negatively affect physical and mental health.

9. Government policies can help create new jobs through investment and innovation.

10. People often choose jobs based on personal passion, income, or job security.

10 Useful Words for IELTS Answers

   I. Employment

  II. Profession

 III. Workforce

 IV. Promotion

  V. Income

 VI. Career

 VII. Recruitment

VIII. Stability

 IX. Unemployment

  X. Motivation

Synonyms / Related Words

- Vocation
- Occupation
- Liveliness

IELTS Writing Task 2 – Q type : Advantage-Disadvantage Outweigh Question-
Some people think that a high salary is more important than job satisfaction. **Do the advantages of a high-paying job outweigh the disadvantages?**

32. Language:

Language is a powerful tool that allows people to express thoughts, share ideas, and connect across cultures. It plays a key role in identity, education, and social integration in both local and global contexts.

10 Points You Can Use in IELTS Answers (Writing/Speaking)

1. Language is essential for communication and the foundation of human interaction.

2. Multilingualism can improve cognitive skills and open up global job opportunities.

3. Language barriers can lead to misunderstandings and limit access to services.

4. English is often considered a global language due to its wide use in business and education.

5. Preserving endangered languages helps maintain cultural heritage and diversity.

6. Learning a new language can enhance memory and problem-solving abilities.

7. Immigrants often face challenges in adapting to a new language and culture.

8. Language plays a vital role in national identity and unity.

9. Digital tools and apps have made language learning more accessible than ever.

10. Governments may promote official languages while supporting minority languages for inclusiveness.

10 Useful Words for IELTS Answers

   I. Communication

  II. Bilingual

 III. Dialect

 IV. Multilingualism

  V. Translation

 VI. Fluency

 VII. Interpretation

VIII. Native speaker

 IX. Literacy

  X. Linguistics

Synonyms / Related Words

- Tongue
- Dialect
- Verbal expression

IELTS Writing Task 2 – Q type : Double Question-
Why is learning a foreign language important? What is the best age to start learning a new language?

33. **Law and Order:**

Law and order are essential for maintaining social stability, protecting citizens, and ensuring justice in society. Without effective legal systems and enforcement, crime can rise and trust in institutions may decline.

10 Points You Can Use in IELTS Answers (Writing/Speaking)

1. Laws provide a framework for acceptable behaviour and help prevent chaos in society.

2. Law enforcement agencies like the police play a crucial role in upholding justice.

3. Strict laws can deter criminal activities and promote public safety.

4. Corruption within the legal system can undermine law and order.

5. Prisons and rehabilitation programs are key components of criminal justice.

6. Fair legal processes ensure that everyone is treated equally under the law.

7. Citizens have a responsibility to follow the law and respect legal institutions.

8. Some believe that harsher punishments reduce crime, while others favour rehabilitation.

9. Technology like surveillance and AI is increasingly used in maintaining law and order.

10. Public awareness and education about laws help build a more law-abiding society.

10 Useful Words for IELTS Answers

I. Justice

II. Crime

III. Enforcement

IV. Legislation

V. Penalty

VI. Deterrent

VII. Authority

VIII. Regulation

IX. Discipline

X. Jurisdiction

Synonyms / Related Words

- Legal system
- Regulation
- Violation

IELTS Writing Task 2 – Q type : Problem-Solution Question-
In some countries, there has been a noticeable rise in crime rates, leading to concerns about the breakdown of law and order.
What are the main causes of this trend, and what solutions can be implemented to address it?

34. **Media:**

Media plays a powerful role in shaping public opinion, spreading information, and influencing societal values. With the rise of digital platforms, media has become more accessible, but concerns about misinformation and bias have also increased.
10 Points You Can Use in IELTS Answers (Writing/Speaking)

1. Media is a key source of news and current events for most people worldwide.

2. Social media platforms allow individuals to share information and express opinions freely.

3. Traditional media, such as television and newspapers, still play a significant role in journalism.

4. Sensationalism and biased reporting can mislead the public and create distrust.

5. Freedom of the press is vital for a healthy democracy.

6. Media can educate people on social, political, and environmental issues.

7. The rise of fake news has made it harder to verify credible sources.

8. Governments sometimes regulate media to control content or protect national interests.

9. Advertising and consumerism are heavily driven by media exposure.

10. Media literacy is essential to help people critically evaluate the information they consume.

10 Useful Words for IELTS Answers

I. Journalism

II. Broadcasting

III. Misinformation

IV. Censorship

V. Bias

VI. Credibility

VII. Influence

VIII. Freedom

IX. Public opinion

X. Platform

Synonyms / Related Words

- Mass communication
- Reporting
- Bulletins

IELTS Writing Task 2 – Q type : Single Opinion Question with Example-

Do you think the media influences people's opinions more positively or negatively? **Give reasons for your answer and include examples from your own experience.**

35. **Mental Health:**

Mental health is an essential aspect of overall well-being, affecting how individuals think, feel, and cope with life. Despite its importance, it is often overlooked or stigmatized, leading to serious social and personal consequences.

10 Points You Can Use in IELTS Answers (Writing/Speaking)

1. Mental health issues such as anxiety and depression are increasingly common worldwide.

2. Stress from work, academic pressure, and social expectations can negatively impact mental health.

3. Early intervention and access to professional support are key to effective treatment.

4. Social stigma often prevents people from seeking help for mental health problems.

5. Mental health awareness campaigns can promote understanding and reduce discrimination.

6. Schools and workplaces are starting to offer mental health support services.

7. A healthy lifestyle, including regular exercise and sleep, can improve mental well-being.

8. Isolation and loneliness are significant contributors to poor mental health.

9. Technology and social media can both support and harm mental health depending on use.

10. Government investment in mental health services is essential for a healthy society.

10 Useful Words for IELTS Answers

I. Anxiety

II. Depression

III. Stigma

IV. Therapy

V. Well-being

VI. Awareness

VII. Support

VIII. Resilience

IX. Isolation

X. Counselling

Synonyms / Related Words

- Emotional health
- Cognitive health
- Counselling

IELTS Writing Task 2 – Q type : To What Extent Do You Agree or Disagree Question-
Mental health is just as important as physical health, and governments should allocate equal funding to both.
To what extent do you agree or disagree with this statement?

36. **Mobile Phones:**

Mobile phones have become an indispensable part of modern life, offering instant communication, entertainment, and access to information. However, excessive use can lead to negative effects such as distraction, addiction, and reduced face-to-face interaction.
10 Points You Can Use in IELTS Answers (Writing/Speaking)

1. Mobile phones allow people to stay connected with friends, family, and work at all times.

2. Smartphones support a wide range of functions, from banking to health tracking.

3. Overuse of mobile phones can lead to issues like poor sleep and eye strain.

4. Mobile phones are often blamed for reducing attention spans, especially among youth.

5. They play a crucial role in emergencies by enabling quick communication.

6. Mobile apps have made education, navigation, and online shopping more accessible.

7. Excessive screen time can affect mental health and increase stress.

8. Mobile phones can be a distraction in schools and workplaces.

9. They contribute to social isolation despite being a tool for communication.

10. Regulations are sometimes needed to control phone use while driving or in public spaces.

10 Useful Words for IELTS Answers

I. Connectivity

II. Addiction

III. Distraction

IV. Accessibility

V. Screen time

VI. Convenience

VII. Communication

VIII. Smartphone

IX. Innovation

X. Dependency

Synonyms / Related Words

- Smart phone

- Cell phone
- Over dependency

IELTS Writing Task 2 – Q type : Advantage-Disadvantage Question-
Mobile phones have both positive and negative impacts on modern society. What are the advantages and disadvantages of using mobile phones?

37. **Music:**

Music is a universal language that transcends borders, cultures, and generations, offering emotional expression and connection. It plays a vital role in entertainment, education, and even mental well-being.
10 Points You Can Use in IELTS Answers (Writing/Speaking)

1. Music can influence mood, reduce stress, and promote relaxation.

2. Different cultures have unique musical traditions that reflect their history and values.

3. Learning to play an instrument enhances memory and coordination.

4. Music is widely used in films, advertising, and therapy for its emotional impact.

5. The digital age has made music more accessible through streaming platforms.

6. Live concerts bring communities together and support the entertainment industry.

7. Some believe music improves concentration and productivity while studying or working.

8. Lyrics in music can shape social attitudes and raise awareness of social issues.

9. Music education in schools supports creativity and emotional development in children.

10. Excessive commercialization of music may reduce artistic quality and originality.

10 Useful Words for IELTS Answers

I. Harmony

II. Rhythm

III. Genre

IV. Instrument

V. Performance

VI. Creativity

VII. Expression

VIII. Tradition

IX. Therapy

X. Streaming

Synonyms / Related Words

- Melody
- Composition
- Track

IELTS Writing Task 2 – Q type : Opinion Question with Example-
Some people think music is purely a form of entertainment, while others believe it has a deeper emotional and cultural significance.
What is your opinion? Use examples from your own experience to support your answer.

38. **Parenting:**

Parenting plays a critical role in shaping a child's values, behavior, and emotional development. Effective parenting requires a balance of love, discipline, and guidance to prepare children for adulthood.

10 Points You Can Use in IELTS Answers (Writing/Speaking)

1. Parenting styles greatly influence a child's self-esteem and academic performance.

2. Positive parenting fosters emotional security and strong parent-child bonds.

3. Strict or authoritarian parenting may lead to fear and reduced communication.

4. Modern parents face challenges like screen time, peer pressure, and work-life balance.

5. Parental involvement in education is linked to better student outcomes.

6. Role modeling is a powerful method through which children learn values and behavior.

7. Inconsistent discipline can confuse children and undermine authority.

8. Single parenting can be demanding but also rewarding with the right support.

9. Societal and cultural expectations often shape parenting approaches.

10. Parenting education programs can help new parents manage responsibilities more effectively.

10 Useful Words for IELTS Answers

I. Nurturing

II. Discipline

III. Responsibility

IV. Guidance

V. Role model

VI. Bonding

VII. Development

VIII. Communication

IX. Influence

X. Authority

Synonyms / Related Words

- Upbringing
- Nurturing
- Behavioural training

IELTS Writing Task 2 – Q type : Advantage-Disadvantage Opinion Question-

Some people believe strict parenting helps raise successful children, while others think a more relaxed approach is better. **What are the advantages and disadvantages of each parenting style, and which do you prefer?**

39. **Public services:**

Public services such as healthcare, education, transportation, and sanitation are essential for the smooth functioning and well-being of a society. They are typically funded by governments to ensure equal access and improve the quality of life for all citizens.

10 Points You Can Use in IELTS Answers (Writing/Speaking)

1. Public services ensure that basic needs like healthcare and education are accessible to everyone, regardless of income.

2. A reliable public transportation system reduces traffic congestion and pollution.

3. Quality education systems contribute to long-term economic and social development.

4. Public healthcare reduces the burden on individuals during emergencies or illness.

5. Clean water and sanitation services are crucial for maintaining public health.

6. Underfunded or poorly managed public services can lead to inequality and dissatisfaction.

7. Taxation is the primary source of funding for public services.

8. Digitalization of public services can increase efficiency and transparency.

9. Emergency services such as police and fire departments are vital for community safety.

10. Governments must regularly evaluate and improve public services to meet the population's changing needs.

10 Useful Words for IELTS Answers

I. Infrastructure

II. Accessibility

III. Welfare

IV. Funding

V. Equality

VI. Efficiency

VII. Taxpayer

VIII. Governance

IX. Utility

X. Allocation

Synonyms / Related Words

- Government services
- Civic amenities
- Social services

IELTS Writing Task 2 – Q type : Problem-Solution Question-
In many countries, public services like healthcare and education are under strain due to population growth and limited funding. What problems does this cause, and what solutions can governments adopt to address them?

40. **Recycling:**

Recycling is a key environmental practice that helps reduce waste, conserve resources, and protect the planet. As global pollution increases, recycling has become essential for achieving sustainability and minimizing landfill usage.

10 Points You Can Use in IELTS Answers (Writing/Speaking)

1. Recycling reduces the amount of waste sent to landfills and incinerators.

2. It helps conserve natural resources like timber, water, and minerals.

3. Recycling lowers greenhouse gas emissions by reducing the need for raw material processing.

4. Many countries have introduced recycling laws and programs to encourage eco-friendly habits.

5. Public awareness and participation are crucial for successful recycling systems.

6. Recycling can create job opportunities in waste management and processing industries.

7. Sorting waste correctly is a common challenge that affects recycling efficiency.

8. Some materials, like plastic and e-waste, are more difficult to recycle than others.

9. Lack of infrastructure can limit recycling efforts in developing countries.

10. Educating children and communities about recycling can lead to long-term environmental benefits.

10 Useful Words for IELTS Answers

   I. Sustainability

  II. Waste

 III. Conservation

 IV. Emissions

  V. Landfill

 VI. Resources

VII. Eco-friendly

VIII. Awareness

IX. Infrastructure

X. Pollution

Synonyms / Related Words

- Reusing
- Repurposing
- Environmental responsibility

IELTS Writing Task 2 – Q type : To What Extent Do You Agree or Disagree Question-
Some people believe that making recycling compulsory by law is the only way to ensure it is taken seriously.
To what extent do you agree or disagree with this statement?

41. **Religion:**

Religion plays a significant role in shaping cultural values, moral beliefs, and social behavior across societies. While it can foster unity and a sense of purpose, it can also be a source of conflict when beliefs differ.
10 Points You Can Use in IELTS Answers (Writing/Speaking)

1. Religion often provides moral guidance and ethical frameworks for individuals.

2. Religious practices and festivals are integral parts of cultural heritage.

3. In many communities, religion supports social cohesion and charity work.

4. Religious freedom is considered a fundamental human right in democratic societies.

5. Conflicts sometimes arise when religious beliefs clash with modern laws or other faiths.

6. Some people argue that religion should be separate from government policies.

7. Religion can influence education systems and social norms.

8. Interfaith dialogue promotes tolerance and understanding among diverse groups.

9. The role of religion is declining in some societies but growing in others.

10. Religious symbols and attire often spark debates on freedom of expression and secularism.

10 Useful Words for IELTS Answers

I. Faith

II. Belief

III. Worship

IV. Tolerance

V. Ritual

VI. Conflict

VII. Morality

VIII. Spirituality

IX. Doctrine

X. Secularism

Synonyms / Related Words

- Faith

- Belief system
- Spirituality

IELTS Writing Task 2 – Q type : Double Question-
What role does religion play in modern society? How can religious differences be managed to promote social harmony?

42. **Science and technology:**

Science and technology have revolutionized every aspect of human life, from healthcare and communication to transportation and education. While they drive innovation and progress, they also raise concerns about privacy, ethics, and environmental impact.
10 Points You Can Use in IELTS Answers (Writing/Speaking)

1. Technological advances have greatly improved medical treatments and increased life expectancy.

2. Science contributes to solving global challenges such as climate change and food security.

3. The rise of artificial intelligence and automation is reshaping the job market.

4. Digital communication tools have made global connectivity faster and easier.

5. There is growing concern over data privacy and surveillance in tech-driven societies.

6. Scientific research drives innovation in industries such as space, energy, and biotechnology.

7. Overreliance on technology can reduce human interaction and critical thinking.

8. Ethical debates often emerge around issues like cloning, genetic engineering, and robotics.

9. Technology in education allows for remote learning and personalized teaching methods.

10. Not all regions have equal access to technological advancements, leading to a digital divide.

10 Useful Words for IELTS Answers

I. Innovation

II. Advancement

III. Automation

IV. Research

V. Development

VI. Efficiency

VII. Ethics

VIII. Connectivity

IX. Surveillance

X. Accessibility

Synonyms / Related Words

- Innovation
- Scientific Advancement
- Technological process

IELTS Writing Task 2 – Q type : Agree/Disagree with Example Question-
Some people believe that technology has made people more isolated. **Do you agree or disagree with this view? Support your answer with relevant**

reasons examples.

43. **Social Media:**

Social media has transformed the way people communicate, share information, and engage with the world. While it offers numerous benefits like global connectivity and self-expression, it also brings challenges such as cyberbullying, misinformation, and addiction.

10 Points You Can Use in IELTS Answers (Writing/Speaking)

1. Social media connects people globally, fostering relationships across borders.

2. It allows users to share opinions, news, and creative content instantly.

3. Many businesses rely on social media for advertising and customer engagement.

4. Platforms like Twitter and Instagram can influence public opinion and social movements.

5. Excessive use of social media is linked to mental health issues like anxiety and low self-esteem.

6. Fake news and misinformation spread quickly on social media networks.

7. Privacy concerns arise due to data tracking and lack of regulation.

8. Social media can distract students and reduce productivity in the workplace.

9. It provides a platform for marginalized voices to be heard.

10. Parental supervision and digital literacy are vital to ensure safe use among children and teenagers.

10 Useful Words for IELTS Answers

I. Connectivity

II. Engagement

III. Influence

IV. Misinformation

V. Privacy

VI. Addiction

VII. Networking

VIII. Platform

IX. Cyberbullying

X. Awareness

Synonyms / Related Words

- Online platforms
- Digital space
- Social networks

IELTS Writing Task 2 – Q type : Advantage-Disadvantage Outweigh Question-

Social media is considered by some to be a powerful tool for communication, while others see it as a harmful influence on society. **What are the advantages and disadvantages of social media, and do you think its benefits outweigh the drawbacks?**

44. **Social Welfare:**

Social welfare refers to government programs and policies designed to support the well-being of vulnerable individuals and communities. It plays a crucial role in reducing poverty, ensuring equality, and promoting social justice.

10 Points You Can Use in IELTS Answers (Writing/Speaking)

1. Social welfare provides financial support to the unemployed, elderly, and disabled.

2. It helps reduce income inequality and bridge the gap between rich and poor.

3. Welfare programs promote equal access to healthcare, education, and housing.

4. Well-managed social welfare systems can boost overall economic stability.

5. Critics argue that welfare may create dependency and reduce motivation to work.

6. Government funding is essential to sustain long-term social welfare services.

7. Welfare benefits often reflect a country's values and commitment to human rights.

8. Misuse and fraud in welfare systems can strain public resources.

9. Conditional welfare, like job training, can encourage self-reliance.

10. Strong welfare systems often correlate with lower crime rates and better health outcomes.

10 Useful Words for IELTS Answers

I. Poverty

II. Equity

III. Subsidy

IV. Unemployment

V. Entitlement

VI. Assistance

VII. Dependence

VIII. Redistribution

IX. Empowerment

X. Social justice

Synonyms / Related Words

- Government aid
- Social support
- Public assistance

IELTS Writing Task 2 – Q type : Problem-Solution Question-
Many governments struggle to provide effective social welfare programs for all citizens. What problems are caused by inadequate social welfare systems, and what solutions can be implemented to improve them?

45. **Sports:**

Sports play an essential role in promoting physical fitness, discipline, and teamwork among individuals of all ages. They also serve as a powerful tool for national pride, social unity, and international cooperation.
10 Points You Can Use in IELTS Answers (Writing/Speaking)

1. Sports encourage a healthy lifestyle and help reduce the risk of chronic diseases.

2. Team sports teach valuable life skills like cooperation, leadership, and communication.

3. International sporting events promote cultural exchange and diplomacy.

4. Sports can be a career path, generating income and recognition for talented athletes.

5. Hosting major sports events can boost a country's economy and tourism industry.

6. Over-commercialization of sports may shift the focus from talent to profit.

7. Gender inequality still exists in many sports in terms of pay and media coverage.

8. School sports programs enhance student engagement and academic performance.

9. Use of performance-enhancing drugs is a growing issue in competitive sports.

10. Investment in community sports facilities increases participation and social well-being.

10 Useful Words for IELTS Answers

  I. Competition

 II. Fitness

III. Discipline

IV. Endurance

 V. Performance

VI. Teamwork

VII. Sponsorship

VIII. Recreation

IX. Athletics

X. Participation

Synonyms / Related Words

- Athletics
- Conditioning
- Physical activities

IELTS Writing Task 2 – Q type : Opinion Question -
Some people believe that sports are essential for physical health, while others think they are more important for developing social and teamwork skills.
Discuss both sides and give your opinion.

46. **Taxes:**

Taxes are a vital source of government revenue used to fund public services such as healthcare, education, and infrastructure. While taxation is essential for a functioning society, debates continue over fairness, rates, and the efficiency of tax systems.
10 Points You Can Use in IELTS Answers (Writing/Speaking)

1. Taxes fund essential public services like roads, schools, and hospitals.

2. Progressive tax systems aim to reduce income inequality by taxing higher earners more.

3. Tax evasion and avoidance undermine government revenue and social trust.

4. Small businesses often struggle with complex tax regulations.

5. Some believe high taxes discourage investment and economic growth.

6. Governments use tax policies to influence behavior, such as taxing cigarettes or sugary drinks.

7. Digital businesses pose new challenges for traditional tax systems.

8. Transparency and accountability in how taxes are spent are critical for public trust.

9. International cooperation is needed to prevent tax avoidance by multinational corporations.

10. Tax incentives can stimulate innovation and environmentally friendly practices.

10 Useful Words for IELTS Answers

I. Revenue

II. Evasion

III. Infrastructure

IV. Progressive

V. Compliance

VI. Inequality

VII. Incentives

VIII. Policy

IX. Accountability

X. Expenditure

Synonyms / Related Words

- Levies
- Duties
- Tariffs

IELTS Writing Task 2 – Q type : Agree/disagree question-
Some people believe that paying taxes is the most important responsibility of a citizen. **Do you agree or disagree with this statement? Give reasons and examples.**

1. **Television :**

Television remains one of the most influential forms of mass media, offering entertainment, education, and information to audiences worldwide. Despite the rise of digital platforms, TV continues to shape public opinion and daily routines across generations.

10 Points You Can Use in IELTS Answers (Writing/Speaking)

1. Television provides educational programs that inform viewers about science, history, and current events.

2. It is a major source of entertainment, offering movies, sports, and reality shows.

3. TV news channels help people stay informed about national and international affairs.

4. Excessive screen time can negatively impact physical and mental health.

5. Children can be influenced by violent or inappropriate content on TV.

6. Public broadcasting offers unbiased, educational, and cultural programming.

7. Television can promote consumerism through constant advertising.

8. It plays a role in preserving culture by broadcasting local language and traditions.

9. TV can help raise awareness of social issues such as poverty or climate change.

10. The rise of streaming services is changing traditional TV viewing habits.

10 Useful Words for IELTS Answers

I. Broadcast

II. Entertainment

III. Advertisement

IV. Viewer

V. Screen time

VI. Programming

VII. Influence

VIII. Commercial

IX. Channel

X. Audience

Synonyms / Related Words

- Broadcast
- Media
- Stream

IELTS Writing Task 2 – Q type : Cause and Effect Question-
Why do people spend so much time watching television, and what effects does this have on individuals and society?

2. **Traditional v/s modern (education/public facilities/culture) :**

The debate between traditional and modern approaches spans education, culture, and public services, reflecting changing values and societal development. While traditional methods often preserve identity and discipline, modern systems focus on efficiency, inclusivity, and innovation.

10 Points You Can Use in IELTS Answers (Writing/Speaking)

1. Traditional education emphasizes rote learning and discipline, whereas modern education promotes creativity and critical thinking.

2. Modern public facilities often use smart technology for efficiency and user convenience.

3. Traditional cultures offer a sense of identity, heritage, and continuity.

4. Some people argue that modern culture is eroding values and weakening social ties.

5. Modern infrastructure tends to be more accessible and inclusive than traditional systems.

6. There is a growing interest in blending traditional wisdom with modern practices (e.g., in medicine or architecture).

7. Traditional ceremonies and festivals strengthen community bonds.

8. Technological advancements in modern education enable distance learning and global collaboration.

9. Traditional systems may resist change, which can hinder progress in a fast-paced world.

10. Balancing tradition and modernity is essential for sustainable cultural and social development.

10 Useful Words for IELTS Answers

I. Heritage

II.   Innovation

III.   Modernization

IV.   Preservation

V.   Inclusivity

VI.   Custom

VII.   Efficiency

VIII.   Transformation

IX.   Tradition

X.   Advancement

Synonyms / Related Words

- Conventional
- Ancestral
- Heritage

IELTS Writing Task 2 – Q type : Advantage-Disadvantage Opinion Question-

Some people think modern methods of education and public services are more effective, while others believe that traditional approaches still have value. **What are the advantages and disadvantages of each, and what is your opinion?**

3.   **Traffic:**

Traffic congestion is a growing issue in urban areas, causing delays, stress, and environmental damage. As cities expand and vehicle ownership rises, managing traffic efficiently has become a pressing public concern.

10 Points You Can Use in IELTS Answers (Writing/Speaking)

1. Increasing car ownership is a primary cause of urban traffic congestion.

2. Public transportation systems can reduce traffic volume and pollution.

3. Poor road planning and maintenance contribute to bottlenecks and slowdowns.

4. Traffic jams lead to loss of productivity and economic inefficiency.

5. Air and noise pollution caused by traffic negatively impact health.

6. Many cities have introduced congestion charges to limit vehicle use in busy zones.

7. Traffic laws and enforcement vary significantly across countries.

8. Smart traffic lights and GPS systems can improve traffic flow.

9. Carpooling and ride-sharing are sustainable alternatives to reduce vehicle numbers.

10. Governments should invest in pedestrian-friendly infrastructure and cycling lanes.

10 Useful Words for IELTS Answers

I.   Congestion

II. Infrastructure

III. Emissions

IV. Commute

V.   Gridlock

VI. Sustainability

VII. Urbanization

VIII. Bottleneck

IX. Regulation

X. Transportation

Synonyms / Related Words

- Transit
- Road Movement
- Gridlock

IELTS Writing Task 2 – Q type : Problem–Solution Question-
Traffic congestion is becoming a major concern in many cities around the world. **What are the main causes of this problem, and what solutions can be proposed to address it?**

4. **Transportation :**

Transportation plays a crucial role in connecting people, goods, and services across regions and nations. With increasing urbanization and globalization, efficient and sustainable transportation systems are more vital than ever.

10 Points You Can Use in IELTS Answers (Writing/Speaking)

1. Public transport systems like buses, trains, and metros reduce traffic congestion and pollution.

2. Private vehicle use contributes to environmental problems and road overcrowding.

3. Air travel facilitates international business and tourism but increases carbon emissions.

4. Investing in cycling infrastructure promotes eco-friendly commuting.

5. Electric vehicles are an emerging solution to reduce fossil fuel dependency.

6. Poor transport systems can limit economic growth and access to education and healthcare.

7. High-speed rail networks can connect major cities efficiently.

8. Government policies can encourage people to shift from cars to public transport.

9. Technological innovations like autonomous vehicles are shaping the future of transport.

10. Rural areas often lack adequate transportation, affecting development and quality of life.

10 Useful Words for IELTS Answers

I. Mobility

II. Infrastructure

III. Emissions

IV. Transit

V. Congestion

VI. Commuting

VII. Accessibility

VIII. Sustainability

IX. Logistics

X. Connectivity

Synonyms / Related Words

- Commutation
- Conveyance
- Transit

IELTS Writing Task 2 – Q type : Advantage–Disadvantage Question-
Many people believe that public transportation should be free of charge.
What are the advantages and disadvantages of this approach?

5. **Travel and tourism:**

Travel and tourism have become a global phenomenon, connecting people across cultures and contributing significantly to economic development. While tourism fosters international understanding, it also raises concerns about sustainability and cultural erosion.
10 Points You Can Use in IELTS Answers (Writing/Speaking)

1. Tourism generates income and employment for local economies.

2. It promotes cultural exchange and global awareness.

3. Popular destinations often suffer from over-tourism and environmental degradation.

4. Ecotourism encourages responsible travel and conservation.

5. Infrastructure improvements often accompany tourism development.

6. Some tourists disrespect local customs or heritage sites.

7. The tourism industry was heavily impacted by the COVID-19 pandemic.

8. Technology has made travel more accessible and affordable.

9. Travel can broaden one's perspective and reduce prejudice.

10. Tourism helps preserve traditional arts and crafts through market demand.

10 Useful Words for IELTS Answers

   I. Destination

  II. Hospitality

 III. Sustainable

 IV. Ecotourism

  V. Economy

 VI. Culture

VII. Attraction

VIII. Conservation

 IX. Heritage

  X. Infrastructure

Synonyms / Related Words

- Hospitality
- Exploration
- Wanderlust

IELTS Writing Task 2 – Q type : Opinion Question with Example-
Some people believe that tourism is beneficial for local communities, while others think it causes harm to their culture and environment. **What is your opinion? Give reasons and examples.**

6. **Unemployment:**

Unemployment remains a critical global issue, affecting economic stability and individual well-being. It can lead to financial hardship, social unrest, and long-term economic decline if not effectively addressed.

10 Points You Can Use in IELTS Answers (Writing/Speaking)

1. High unemployment can lead to poverty and reduced quality of life.

2. It affects mental health, causing stress, anxiety, and loss of purpose.

3. Governments may struggle to provide enough jobs for growing populations.

4. Automation and AI are replacing many manual and routine jobs.

5. Education systems may not align with current job market demands.

6. Youth unemployment is a major concern in many developing countries.

7. Long-term unemployment can reduce a person's chances of being rehired.

8. Job training and upskilling programs can help reduce unemployment rates.

9. Unemployment can lead to increased crime and social tension.

10. Globalization can both create and eliminate jobs depending on the sector.

10 Useful Words for IELTS Answers

I. Jobless

II. Workforce

III. Skill gap

IV. Economy

V. Redundancy

VI. Layoff

VII. Underemployment

VIII. Automation

IX. Labor market

X. Recession

Synonyms / Related Words

- Joblessness
- Labour surplus
- Economic environment

IELTS Writing Task 2 – Q type : Cause and Effect Question-
What are the main causes of unemployment in today's world, and what effects does it have on individuals and society?

7. **Waste Management:**

Waste management is a vital environmental issue that involves the collection, processing, and disposal of waste materials. Effective waste handling is essential to reduce pollution, protect natural resources, and promote sustainable living.
10 Points You Can Use in IELTS Answers (Writing/Speaking)

1. Improper waste disposal contributes to land, water, and air pollution.

2. Recycling and composting are key strategies in modern waste management.

3. Many urban areas face challenges due to growing amounts of household and industrial waste.

4. Plastic waste, in particular, poses a long-term environmental threat.

5. Governments can implement stricter regulations and penalties for littering and illegal dumping.

6. Public awareness and education campaigns can promote better waste practices.

7. Waste-to-energy technologies convert trash into usable energy.

8. Developing countries often lack the infrastructure for efficient waste management.

9. Businesses are increasingly adopting eco-friendly packaging to reduce waste.

10. Segregating waste at the source (organic, recyclable, hazardous) can improve overall management.

10 Useful Words for IELTS Answers

1. Landfill

2. Recycling

3. Disposal

4. Sustainability

5. Compost

6. Incineration

7. Pollution

8. Biodegradable

9. Regulation

10. Hazardous

Synonyms / Related Words

- Waste disposal
- Refuse control
- Contamination

IELTS Writing Task 2 – Q type : Problem–Solution Question-
Improper waste management has become a serious environmental issue in many parts of the world. **What are the main problems caused by this, and what solutions can be implemented to address them?**

8. **Water:**

Water is an essential natural resource crucial for sustaining life, agriculture, and industry. However, increasing demand, pollution, and climate change are threatening global water availability and quality.
10 Points You Can Use in IELTS Answers (Writing/Speaking)

1. Freshwater scarcity is a growing concern in many regions of the world.

2. Industrial and agricultural pollution contaminate vital water sources.

3. Climate change is disrupting rainfall patterns, affecting water availability.

4. Access to clean drinking water is still limited in developing countries.

5. Overuse of water in households and farming leads to depletion.

6. Water conservation methods like rainwater harvesting can help reduce waste.

7. Desalination is a potential solution, though it's expensive and energy-intensive.

8. Education and awareness are key to promoting water-saving habits.

9. Governments must invest in sustainable water infrastructure and management.

10. Clean water is crucial for public health and disease prevention.

10 Useful Words for IELTS Answers

I. Scarcity

II. Contamination

III. Conservation

IV. Irrigation

V. Hydration

VI. Sustainability

VII. Depletion

VIII. Infrastructure

IX. Sanitation

X. Renewable

Synonyms / Related Words

- Preservation
- Protection
- Hydration

IELTS Writing Task 2 – Q type : Advantage–Disadvantage Opinion Question-

Some people believe that making water a paid commodity is the best way to encourage its conservation, while others think water should always be free and accessible. **What are the advantages and disadvantages of this**

approach, and what is your opinion?

9. **Weapons:**

Weapons, ranging from conventional arms to advanced nuclear technology, play a significant role in national security and global politics. However, their misuse can lead to devastating conflicts, mass destruction, and long-term instability.

10 Points You Can Use in IELTS Answers (Writing/Speaking)

1. Weapons are essential for defense and maintaining national sovereignty.

2. The global arms trade is a major economic sector.

3. Misuse of weapons leads to crime, violence, and civilian casualties.

4. Nuclear weapons act as a deterrent but pose existential threats.

5. Stricter gun control laws are debated in many countries.

6. Armed conflicts often escalate due to easy access to firearms.

7. Technological advancement has led to more precise yet deadlier weapons.

8. Disarmament efforts aim to promote global peace and security.

9. Military spending on weapons can divert funds from education and healthcare.

10. International treaties like the Non-Proliferation Treaty attempt to regulate weapon use.

10 Useful Words for IELTS Answers

I. Armament

II. Firearms

III. Disarmament

IV. Deterrent

V. Arsenal

VI. Militarization

VII. Conflict

VIII. Security

IX. Regulation

X. Escalation

Synonyms / Related Words

- Firearms
- Ammunitions
- Combat

IELTS Writing Task 2 – Q type : To What Extent Do You Agree/ Disagree Question-
Some people believe that the possession of weapons promotes peace through deterrence, while others think it increases the likelihood of conflict. **To what extent do you agree or disagree with this statement?**

10. **Work:**

Work plays a central role in people's lives by providing income, purpose, and social identity. However, the changing nature of employment due to technology and globalization is reshaping how and where people work.
10 Points You Can Use in IELTS Answers (Writing/Speaking)

1. A stable job provides financial security and supports personal development.

2. Work-life balance is becoming increasingly important in modern careers.

3. Remote work and freelancing have become more common since the pandemic.

4. Job satisfaction is often linked to meaningful tasks and recognition.

5. Technological automation is reducing demand for certain manual jobs.

6. Many workers face pressure due to long hours and high-performance expectations.

7. Professional development and lifelong learning are essential in today's job market.

8. Youth unemployment remains a challenge in many parts of the world.

9. Workplace diversity and inclusion can enhance innovation and productivity.

10. Government policies can influence employment rates and job creation.

10 Useful Words for IELTS Answers

I. Employment

II. Occupation

III. Productivity

IV. Workforce

V. Career

VI. Automation

VII. Job security

VIII. Workplace

IX. Flexibility

X. Promotion

Synonyms / Related Words

- Employment
- Vocation
- Remuneration

IELTS Writing Task 2 – Q type : Double Question with Example-
Many people prioritize high salaries when choosing a job, while others value job satisfaction more. **What are the advantages of each approach, and can you give examples of when one might be more important than the other?**

You have now reached the end of this comprehensive IELTS treasury of topics, having explored 102 essential themes with targeted vocabulary, practical ideas, and question types designed to mirror the real IELTS experience. By working through each topic, you can build a powerful toolkit of language, examples, and structured thinking that will help you approach both Writing Task 2 and the Speaking test with greater clarity and confidence.

But always remember, success in IELTS is not just about memorizing answers, but about being familiar with key issues, knowing how to organize your ideas, and expressing yourself with accuracy and fluency. Return to these topics often, practice forming full essays and speaking responses, and keep expanding your vocabulary and understanding.

With consistent effort, smart preparation, and the insights gained from this book, you are well on your way to achieving the band score you aim for.

Best of luck for your IELTS journey — and beyond!